COOKIES
from Hawai'i's
Kitchen

D1557729

COOKIES
from Hawai'i's Kitchen

Muriel Miura

Photography by Kaz Tanabe

MUTUAL PUBLISHING

Library of Congress Cataloging-in-Publication Data

Miura, Muriel.
  Cookies from Hawaii's kitchen / Muriel Miura ; photography by Kaz Tanabe.
    p. cm.
  Summary: "Over 120 delicious cookie recipes, each with a special island touch. Tips on choosing ingredients, baking techniques, storing, and packaging also included"--Provided by publisher.
  Includes index.
  ISBN-13: 978-1-56647-815-1 (concealed wire-o, hardcover : alk. paper)
  ISBN-10: 1-56647-815-4 (concealed wire-o, hardcover : alk. paper)
  1. Cookies. 2. Baking--Hawaii. I. Title.
TX772.M585 2006
641.8'65409969--dc22

                              2006026677

ISBN-10: 1-56647-815-4
ISBN-13: 978-1-56647-815-1

Design by Emily R. Lee
Photo Art Direction by Jane Gillespie

First Printing, October 2006
Second Printing, June 2007
Third Printing, September 2010

Mutual Publishing, LLC
1215 Center Street, Suite 210
Honolulu, Hawai'i 96816
Ph: (808) 732-1709 / Fax: (808) 734-4094
email: info@mutualpublishing.com
www.mutualpublishing.com

Printed in Korea

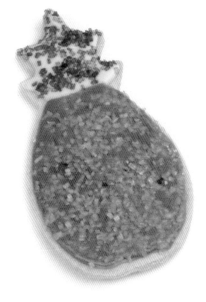

Contents

Foreword viii

Acknowledgments ix

Introduction x

PART I: BAKING GREAT COOKIES: COOKIE BASICS

BEFORE YOU START TO BAKE 2

EQUIPMENT 2

PANS AND PAN PREPARATION 3

BASIC INGREDIENTS 4

MEASURING 5

MIXING 6

BAKING 6

DECORATING 7

STORING 9

PACKAGING 9

FREEZING 10

PACKING FOR MAILING 11

GIFT WRAPPING 11

PART II: SIMPLY COOKIES! RECIPES

BARS & BROWNIES 14

Always popular and baked all at once in a pan

DROP COOKIES 42

Fast and easy to prepare from simple oatmeal to fancy macaroons

PRESSED & SHAPED COOKIES 66
Balls and a variety of fancy shapes for the cookie jar

SLICE & BAKE COOKIES 94
Slice and bake convenience in several flavors

ROLLED & CUT-OUT COOKIES PLUS FROSTINGS 106
*Use a rolling pin, cookie cutters, knives, and pastry wheels
to make special treats—some frosted and decorated*

NO-BAKE COOKIES 124
Easy-to-make and delicious

PART III: APPENDICES
GLOSSARY OF COOKING TERMS 140
PRIMARY COOKIE INGREDIENTS 143
WEIGHTS & MEASURES 148
QUICK SUBSTITUTIONS 149
INDEX OF RECIPES 151

Dedication

To Alissa and Stephen—
Have fun baking great cookies!
With love,
Grandma

and
for cookie lovers everywhere

Foreword

Cookies were originally twice-baked. The cookies dried out so that they kept well—essential in the days before airtight containers were available. In the early days, some cookie batters were baked while some were fried into wafers.

During the Middle Ages, improvements were made and sugar and spices were added to the biscuits making them more palatable. It was during the late Middle Ages that it was discovered that adding beaten egg to biscuit dough made the finished product lighter and that ground nuts could also be used instead of flour…this led to the creation of meringue sponge and macaroon cookies.

During the 18th and 19th century, cookie mixtures changed greatly and enriched shortcakes became very popular. These rich, buttery kinds of dough still form the basis of many cookies today. During the 19th century, cheaper sugar and flour became available as well as chemical raising agents such as baking soda. As a result, cookie factories were able to open up to serve the public. As factory-made cookies improved, more people began to buy their cookies rather than bake their own.

However, in recent years, consumers have started to turn away from foods containing artificial additives and commercial cookies are becoming less popular…there has been a resurgence in home-baked products.

Time-saving kitchen equipment and devices have helped speed up cookie baking, and the availability of more unusual ingredients has opened up the possibilities for today's cook to make just about any cookie desired…thus, the birth of this cookbook. With the help of this book, you'll learn some basic techniques plus have a nice array of traditional as well as contemporary cookie recipes. You'll enjoy baking your own cookies more than ever!

Acknowledgments

· ·

A heartfelt gratitude to all those who contributed to my collection of cookie recipes during my long career as an educator and home economist. This book of cookie recipes represents the contribution of many family, friends, colleagues, and acquaintances and the culmination of countless individual efforts.

I would be remiss if I didn't thank my Maryland family for their encouragement and support, especially to my daughter, Shari, for sharing her thoughts, ideas and recipes for this book. And, as always, to my husband, Yoshi, for his continued support and patience.

My sincerest thanks to my Mutual Publishing family. This book would never have been published had it not been for their expertise, dedication, support, and hard work…especially

Bennett Hymer for his friendship, faith, and confidence in my work
Gay Wong for her assistance, support, and friendship
Jane Gillespie for her expertise in production
Emily Lee for her layout skills
Lani Miyahara for proofreading
Nicole Sakai for her assistance
Sean Nagamatsu for his assistance
Holly Hayashi
Sally Watanabe
Sam Choy
Malia & Jade Ogoshi
Keenan Ohta

Introduction

Cookies! Crisp, flaky, chewy, plain, frosted, decorated, sweet, or tart—they come in all shapes, sizes, and flavors, and are loved by everyone. Ever since the Dutch introduced *koekjes* to the New World, Americans have been wild about cookies. The first cookies were actually tiny cakes baked as a test to ensure the right oven temperature for large cakes. Obviously, someone liked the results of the test. A freshly baked, soft, warm cookie right out of the oven is among the best-loved foods, enjoyed by young and old alike.

My grandchildren love cookies, as do most children, so whenever possible, they join in the baking fun (under careful supervision, of course). They love the process of making cookies, particularly getting covered in flour, sampling the cookie dough, rolling out the dough, making interesting cookie shapes, and decorating them with frosting, sprinkles, and colored sugar.

Cookies are made in many different ways: bars, drop, pressed and shaped, sliced and baked, rolled and cut-out, for example. Although brownies and blondies are not considered to be cookies by some, they are a variation of cookie bars or little cakes. Recipes for all of these varieties are included in this book.

It has been fun compiling all kinds of cookie recipes from traditional to contemporary. There were so many amazing recipes to choose from that it was challenging to select the best for inclusion in this cookbook.

As long as you have good, reliable recipes and the best ingredients, it's quite simple to make 'onolicious cookies. This cookie cookbook gives no one any excuse to put off baking a batch. Whatever your level of culinary expertise, the technique for cookie baking is easy and the equipment minimal so once you start baking, expect to have your cookie jars and containers full!

Even the most accomplished cookie baker will appreciate some of my special cookie baking tips. Make the most of your time in the kitchen with these helpful hints on preparing, baking, and storing all kinds of cookies.

Part of the joy of cookies is their versatility. You'll find new, unusual recipes as well as traditional favorites that can be eaten anytime whether it is after-school snacking or as a dessert when entertaining. May this collection be a treasury of cookie recipes you will enjoy and cherish for years.

Happy baking!

Muriel Miura, CFCS

PART 1

BAKING GREAT COOKIES

COOKIE BASICS

BEFORE YOU START TO BAKE

- Read recipe carefully.
- Preheat your oven twenty minutes before baking.
- Assemble all your ingredients—saves time and steps.
- Gather all the utensils you will be using.
- Measure ingredients carefully using standard cups and spoons.
- Use the pan size that the recipe states.

EQUIPMENT

- Wooden spoons, large and medium
- Rubber scraper or spatula, large and small
- Wide spatula for transferring cookies to rack from baking sheets
- Standard glass measuring cup for liquid ingredients
- Rimless dry measuring cup (1 cup line is even with top)
- Set of graduated measuring cups (1/4, 1/3, 1/2, 1 cup)
- Set of measuring spoons (1/4, 1/2, 1 teaspoon, 1 tablespoon)
- Set of mixing bowls
- Rolling pin
- Straight edge knife or spatula for "leveling off" ingredients
- Cookie cutters
- Shiny insulated cookie/baking sheets without sides
- Jelly roll pan
- Square pan, 2 to 2-1/2 inches deep
- Oblong pan, 1-1/2 to 2-1/2 inches deep
- Round layer pan, 1-1/4 × 8-inch pan; 1-1/2 × 9-inch pan
- Wire or wood cooling rack(s)

- Cookie decorating utensils
- Soft pastry brush
- Pastry bag fitted with decorating tips, optional
- Cookie press, optional
- Wire strainer or sifter for powdered sugar

PANS & PAN PREPARATION

- Use shiny, insulated cookie sheets to help prevent cookies from becoming too dark on the bottom. Cookies baked on insulated baking sheets may take longer to bake. If baking sheet has four sides, cookies may not brown as evenly…use baking sheets that are open on one to three sides.
- If using a nonstick baking sheet, watch carefully—cookies may brown quickly. Manufacturer's directions may suggest reducing oven temperature by 25°F.
- If cookie sheets are thin, consider using two sheets, stacking one on top of the other for insulation.
- Grease the baking sheet only if directed in the recipe, using solid shortening or nonstick cooking spray. Using butter, margarine, or vegetable oil for greasing will cause the area between the cookies to burn, which will make it difficult to clean.

BASIC INGREDIENTS

- *Flour* is pre-sifted today so sifting is not necessary. Use all-purpose flour for most cookies; when using whole-wheat flour, substitute it for half the amount of all-purpose flour to prevent dryness. Too much flour makes cookies dry and tough; too little flour causes them to spread and lose their shape.
- *Sugar* adds sweetness and color and contributes to spreading. The higher the sugar-to-flour ratio in a recipe, the more tender and crisp the cookies.
- *Liquids* tend to make cookies crisper by making them spread more during baking.
- *Fats* add flavor to cookies and make them tender. *Margarine and butter* both produce a crisper cookie than hydrogenated shortening and can be used interchangeably. Butter makes a crisper cookie than margarine does and gives a better flavor. *Shortening* gives cookies a soft, moist texture and is often used for fruit bars and soft drop cookies. Do not directly substitute vegetable oil for solid fat.
- *Eggs* add richness, moisture, and structure to cookies. However, too many eggs make cookies tough and crumbly.

MEASURING

- *Flour*–Spoon flour lightly into a "dry" measuring cup…heap it up then level off cup with straight-edged knife. Do not shake cup.
- *Sugar*–Needs sifting only if lumpy. Spoon lightly into "dry" measuring cup; level it off with a straight-edged knife. Do not tap cup.
- *Brown Sugar*–Press through coarse sieve if lumpy or crush lumps with rolling pin. Pack into "dry" measuring cup just enough to hold its shape then level off with straight-edged knife.
- *Powdered Sugar*–Press through sieve or sift to remove lumps. Spoon lightly into "dry" measuring cup; level off with straight-edged knife. Do not tap cup.
- *Shortening*–Use graduated measuring cups. Pack shortening at room temperature into measuring cup. Level off with straight-edged knife. In measuring less than 1/4 cup, use a tablespoon.
- *Baking Powder, Baking Soda, Salt, Cornstarch, Spices, Cream of Tartar, Etc.*–Fill measuring spoon then level off with straight-edged knife.

- *Liquids*–Use a glass measuring cup. Pour liquid into cup on table. Have measuring line at eye level.
- *Eggs*–They vary in size so it is best to measure them. Never use less than the minimum amount specified in the recipe.
  2 medium eggs = 1/3 cup
  2 large eggs = 1/2 cup
  3 medium eggs = 1/2 cup
  3 large eggs = 2/3 cup

MIXING

- Fats, sugars, and liquids are usually mixed together first, either by an electric mixer or by hand, until all ingredients are well combined. The dry ingredients are then stirred into the creamed mixture by hand, usually just until moistened.
- Overmixing the cookie dough will result in tough cookies.
- Use fresh butter for best results. Let stand at room temperature until it's malleable, but not too soft, about 30 to 45 minutes depending on the room temperature.
- Use room-temperature eggs.
- Use pre-sifted all-purpose flour unless specified otherwise.
- Look for smooth mixture when creaming butter and sugar.

BAKING

- Make sure your oven is properly calibrated.
- Preheat oven at least twenty minutes before baking.
- Use shiny, heavy-gauge, or insulated cookie sheets with low or no sides.
- Line cookie sheet with parchment.
- Make cookies the same size and thickness for uniform baking.
- Set cookie dough far enough apart to allow for spreading.
- Place cookie sheet in the center of the oven.
- Check for doneness at the minimum baking time given.
- Unless recipe states otherwise, remove baked cookies immediately from the baking sheet with a wide spatula and place on wire rack to cool completely.

DECORATING

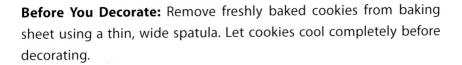

Decorator's Tools:
- Several sizes of decorating bags
- Accompanying decorating bag tips
- Cookie stamps
- Cookie cutters
- Stencils
- Paint brushes for adding detailed markings
- Decorator sugars
- Assorted sprinkle decorations like stars, nonpareils, rainbow, and colored sugars

Before You Decorate: Remove freshly baked cookies from baking sheet using a thin, wide spatula. Let cookies cool completely before decorating.

Piping with Decorating Bag: Fill the bag with icing, then hold tip at an angle. Using even pressure, squeeze bag while directing tip to where design should go.

Paste Food Coloring: Since paste coloring is very vibrant, put a small amount at a time into the icing. Mix it well, using less than you think you'll need at the beginning; add more as desired.

Ways of Decorating:
- Stenciling with colored sugar or sifted powdered sugar.
- Chocolate trims with chocolate sprinkles or chocolate curls (draw a vegetable peeler at an angle across room-temperature chocolate bars.

- Candy trims are easy and sweeter. Try sliced gumdrops and red cinnamon candy or crushed peppermint for a colorful finish.
- Painting with cocoa paint (equal parts unsweetened cocoa powder and water) on glazed baked cookies. Or, brush egg paint (1 egg yolk, 1 teaspoon water and food coloring) on unbaked cookies and bake.
- Two-color glaze by spooning one color of icing evenly over the cookie surface then add small amount of a second color; use toothpick to "pull" the icing and make a design.
- Dips and drizzles are nice and easy. Melt 6 ounces of chocolate with 2 teaspoons shortening; dip half or all of each cooled cookie in the melted mixture or drizzle it over the tops of the cookies.

STORING

Cool cookies thoroughly before storing. Slide baked cookies onto wire cake racks with spatula. Do not overlap or stack cookies until cooled. Store just one kind of cookie in a container; they will all taste the same if they are mixed.

Bars: Store in an airtight container or in the pan in which they are baked. Cover the pan tightly with self-lid or aluminum foil.

Crisp Cookies: Store in a loosely covered container. If they absorb moisture from the air, crisp them in a slow oven (300°F) for about 5 minutes. Cool. Avoid storing with soft cookies as they will turn soft.

Soft Cookies: Store in a tightly covered container. Slices of apple or orange, or bread placed in the container will help mellow and moisten the cookies. Change the fruit or bread often.

PACKAGING

The use of clear cellophane packages, approved for food items, is recommended. Place the cookies carefully in the packages and heat-seal to ensure freshness. Make attractive, clearly written labels. Include *name of cookies*, *date of preparation*, *expiration date (if applicable)*, and *special notes*.

FREEZING

Cookies can be frozen up to two months if securely wrapped. Thaw at room temperature.

Baked Cookie Bars: Arrange bars on waxed paper or cardboard. Place in freeze bag, press out as much air as possible; seal, label and freeze. Cookies may also be wrapped in freezer wrap. Press out air, seal, label, and freeze. Thaw 15 minutes before serving.

Other Cookies: Pack gently in freezer box or freezer bags. Press out as much air as possible. Seal, label, and freeze. Thaw 15 minutes before serving.

Cookie Dough: Cookie dough can be wrapped and refrigerated for about 4-5 days or frozen for several weeks. Form refrigerator (ice box) cookie dough into rolls. Wrap in plastic wrap or freezer paper; press out excess air, seal, label, and freeze. Thaw dough in refrigerator about 1 hour or until dough slices easily. Pack other types of cookie dough in freezer containers. Seal, label, and freeze. Thaw overnight in refrigerator or until dough handles easily.

PACKING FOR MAILING

Send only types of cookies that can stand jostling. These include the rich moist bars and the cake-type (soft) drop cookies.

Bars: Line heavy cardboard box (about the size to fit the amount of cookies) with aluminum foil or waxed paper. Cut cookies to fit the box. Do not cut individually. Place foil or waxed paper between layers and on top. Wrap box with corrugated paper or bubble wrap and heavy paper. Mark "PERISHABLE" and "HANDLE WITH CARE."

Cake-type (soft) Cookies: Line sturdy box with aluminum foil or waxed paper. Place crumpled paper or layer of popcorn or sugarcoated cereal in bottom. Wrap cookies in pairs (back to back with waxed paper between) in foil or waxed paper. Pack snugly in rows. Fill crevices with crumpled paper, popcorn, or cereal. Top with layer of aluminum foil or waxed paper and final layer with crumpled paper, popcorn, or cereal. Tap box shut. Wrap and tie securely. Mark "PERISHABLE" and "HANDLE WITH CARE."

GIFT WRAPPING

Containers for homemade cookie gifts:
- Cans of all shapes and sizes
- Strong box neatly covered with pretty wrapping paper or foil
- Baskets of all shapes, sizes, and colors
- New pan, colander, or serving tray
- Glass stemware
- Brightly colored bowls and plates
- Wide-mouth jars with lids

- Cookie jars
- Assorted mugs or oversized latte coffee cups
- Handcrafted gift boxes lined with waxed paper and layers of tissue
- Ready-made bags of paper, cardboard, and cellophane
- Interesting kitchen containers – i.e. bamboo steamer

Finishing Touches:

- Use crumpled paper or polythene granules to keep glass and jars safe.
- Tie a thin string or decorative tape or ribbon around a paper or cotton fabric bag.
- Cover jar tops with a circle of fabric or paper.
- Finish the gift with plenty of ribbons and an attractive card.
- Use colorful and interesting dishtowels or napkins; secure with ribbon to wrap packaged cookies (the Japanese wrap gifts in fabric).
- Attach the recipe to the gift package using colorful tags and ribbons.

PART 2

SIMPLY COOKIES!

RECIPES

BARS &
BROWNIES

Bar cookies and brownies are always popular because they're easy to prepare. Sometimes chewy, sometimes cakey, and sometimes crispy and crunchy, but they are always delicious! These cookies are fast to prepare as they're spread in a pan and baked all at once, rather than being individually shaped. After baking, they may be cut into squares, rectangles, or triangles—or, in some cases, just broken into irregular chunks. They're great for "take-alongs" to picnics, tailgates, and parties—you can wrap and carry them easily right in their baking pans!

Tips for Bars & Brownies

- Use the pan size specified in the recipe. Cookies made in a larger pan will be dry and overbaked; those made in a smaller pan will be underbaked.
- Cut into bars, squares, or triangles when the batch is completely cool unless recipe specifies cutting while warm.
- For easy clean up and to ensure evenly cut bars and brownies, line the pan with foil.
- Use a plastic knife to cut bar cookies easily.
- Cool baked bars in their pan on a wire rack.
- Spread batter or dough evenly into pan.

Apricot-Coconut Bars

Yield: About 24 bars

The tangy flavor of apricot blends amazingly well with coconut in this easy bar cookie.

$3/_4$ cup vegetable shortening
1 cup sugar
1 egg
1 teaspoon vanilla
2 cups flour
$1/_4$ teaspoon salt
$11/_2$ cups shredded coconut
$1/_2$ cup chopped macadamia nuts or pecans
1 (12-ounce) jar apricot jam

Cream together shortening and sugar in mixing bowl until light and fluffy. Beat in egg and vanilla. Stir in flour and salt; mix well. Spread one-half of the flour mixture into a greased 9-inch square baking pan; press slightly. Spread evenly with coconut, nuts, and jam; cover with remaining flour mixture. Bake. Temperature: 350°F. Time: 35 to 40 minutes. Cool in pan; cut into bars to serve.

Banana Bars with Orange Butter Icing

Yield: About 24 bars

My grandchildren love to snack on fresh bananas and this recipe offers another way for banana lovers to enjoy the 'ono fruit.

4 eggs, beaten
2 cups mashed ripe bananas
1²/₃ cups sugar
1 cup vegetable oil
2 cups all-purpose flour
2 teaspoons baking powder
1 teaspoon baking soda
1 teaspoon salt
2 teaspoons ground cinnamon

Orange Butter Icing:
¹/₄ cup butter, softened
3 cups powdered sugar
¹/₄ cup orange juice

In a large bowl, beat together eggs, bananas, sugar, and oil. In a separate bowl, stir together flour, baking powder, baking soda, salt, and cinnamon; add to the banana mixture; mix well. Spread evenly on an ungreased cookie sheet. Bake. Temperature: 350°F. Time: 25 to 30 minutes or until done. Allow to cool.

To prepare Orange Butter Icing, cream butter; add powdered sugar alternately with orange juice and mix until consistency is smooth. Spread on top of Banana Bars and let it set until firm, about 15 to 30 minutes. Cut into squares or rectangles.

Hawaiian Fruit Bars

Yield: About 24 bars

The island state of Hawai'i offers many delicious food items. These fruit bars offer a popular combination of pineapple, coconut, and macadamia nuts.

$1/2$ cup butter or margarine, melted
$1^1/_2$ cups sugar
4 eggs, well-beaten
$1^1/_2$ cups flour
$1/2$ teaspoon baking soda
$1/2$ teaspoon salt
1 can crushed pineapple, well-drained
$1/2$ cup chopped macadamia nuts
$1/2$ cup shredded coconut
2 tablespoons powdered sugar for sprinkling

Mix together melted butter or margarine with sugar and eggs. Add flour, baking soda, and salt; mix well. Mix in pineapple, macadamia nuts, and coconut. Pour mixed batter into greased 9 × 13 × 2-inch pan. Bake. Temperature: 350°F. Time: 30 to 45 minutes. Cool and cut into square or rectangular bars. May be sprinkled with powdered sugar before serving, if desired.

Variations:

Substitute chopped guava rind, pitted Surinam cherries, or chopped mango for coconut.

Above: Hawaiian Fruit Bars

Below: Favorite Brownies (see page 37)

Pineapple Mac Nut Bars

Yield: About 24 bars

Once proclaimed the "king" of fruits in Hawai'i, pineapple is paired with macadamia nuts for a delicious bar cookie.

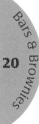
$1/_2$ cup butter or margarine, softened
2 cups sugar
4 eggs
$1^1/_2$ cups flour
$1/_2$ teaspoon baking soda
$1/_2$ teaspoons salt
1 can crushed pineapple, drained well
1 cup chopped macadamia nuts
2 tablespoons powdered sugar

Soften butter or margarine at room temperature. Cream butter or margarine and sugar until light and fluff. Add eggs, one at a time, mixing well after each addition. Combine flour, baking soda, and salt. Add dry ingredients alternately with crushed pineapple to creamed butter mixture. Add nuts; mix well and pour batter into greased and floured 13 × 9 × 2-inch pan. Bake. Temperature: 350°F. Time: 35 to 40 minutes. Cool and sprinkle with powdered sugar. Cut into squares or rectangles.

Variations:
Pineapple Nut Bars: Substitute pecans or walnuts for macadamia nuts.

Toffee Bars

Yield: About 36 bars

For a change, cut these cookies into triangular shapes—bar cookies do not always need to be cut into rectangles.

• •

$^3/_4$ cup butter, softened
$^3/_4$ cup brown sugar, packed
$1^1/_2$ cups flour
$^1/_4$ teaspoon salt

Filling:

1 (14-ounce) can sweetened condensed milk
2 tablespoons butter
$1^1/_2$ teaspoons vanilla extract
2 cups semisweet chocolate pieces
1 cup almond brickle pieces or toasted chopped macadamia nuts

Beat 3/4 cup butter and brown sugar on medium speed in large mixer bowl until well combined. Stir in flour and salt; mix well. With floured hands, press dough into greased 9 × 13 × 2-inch baking pan. Bake. Temperature: 350°F. Time: 18 to 20 minutes or until light brown. Transfer pan to wire rack to cool.

Prepare Filling in medium saucepan by cooking condensed milk and 2 tablespoons butter over medium heat until bubbly, stirring constantly; cook and stir for 5 more minutes or until mixture thickens and becomes smooth. Stir in vanilla. Spread filling over baked crust and bake additional 12 to 15 minutes or until top layer is golden. Sprinkle evenly with chocolate pieces; bake 1 to 2 minutes more or until pieces are shiny and melted. Remove from oven; transfer to wire rack and immediately spread chocolate evenly over baked layer. Sprinkle with brickle pieces or macadamia nuts. Cool. Cover and chill until chocolate is set. Cut into 3 × 2-inch rectangles; cut diagonally into triangles. Store, covered, in refrigerator until ready to serve.

Tsubushian Shortbread

Yield: About 24 bars

Red Azuki Bean Paste Shortbread
The exotic flavor of sweetened red azuki bean paste is combined with a
flaky, light shortbread crust…another tasty cookie treat!

2$^1/_2$ cups flour
1$^1/_2$ cups sugar
1 cup butter or margarine
1 teaspoon baking powder
$^1/_4$ teaspoon salt
3 eggs, slightly beaten
1 cup chopped nuts (macadamia, pecans, walnuts)
1 can (12-ounce) tsubushian (red Azuki bean paste)

In a large bowl, combine 2 cups of the flour and 1/2 cup of the sugar; cut in butter until mealy. Press mixture evenly into 13 × 9 × 2-inch pan. Bake. Temperature: 350°F. Time: 20 minutes. Meanwhile, combine remaining flour, sugar, baking powder, and salt in a medium bowl; mix well. Mix in eggs, nuts, and tsubushian; pour mixture over baked crust and bake additional 40 to 45 minutes. Cut into bars while warm; let stand to cool.

Fruit Bars

Yield: About 4 dozen

You'll want to make some of these fruit-filled bars. These cookies keep well and are more flavorful and moist after a day or two. They take some time to bake but are worth the effort.

. . . .

$1/2$ cup butter or margarine, softened
$1/2$ cup sugar
$1/2$ cup brown sugar, packed
2 eggs, slightly beaten
$1/2$ teaspoon vanilla extract
1 cup whole-wheat flour
$11/4$ cups all-purpose flour
$1/4$ cup toasted wheat germ
$1/4$ teaspoon salt
$1/4$ teaspoon baking soda
Fruit filling of choice (recipes follow)

In large mixer bowl, beat together butter or margarine with sugars until creamy. Beat in eggs and vanilla. In another bowl, stir together whole-wheat and all-purpose flour, wheat germ, salt, and baking soda; gradually add to butter mixture; blend thoroughly. Cover dough tightly with plastic food wrap and refrigerate 1 to 2 hours or until easy to handle. Meanwhile prepare fruit filling of choice; set aside.

Divide dough into 2 equal portions; return one portion to refrigerator. Roll other portion to a straight-edged 9 × 15-inch rectangle on floured board; cut lengthwise into three strips. Divide cooled fruit filling into 6 equal portions and evenly distribute one portion down center of each strip, bringing it out to ends. Use long spatula to lift sides of each dough strip over filling, overlapping edges slightly on top. Press together light- ly. Cut strips in half crosswise; lift and invert onto greased baking sheets, seam side down. Brush off excess flour. Refrigerate 15 to 30 minutes. Meanwhile, repeat rolling and filling with remaining dough. Bake. Temperature: 375°F. Time: 15 to 20 minutes or until golden brown. Cool on baking sheets on rack for 10 minutes; transfer cookies to wire racks and let cool completely. Store in airtight container.

Variations:

Fig Bars: Using a food process, grind together 1 pound dried figs (about 2 cups lightly packed) and 1/2 cup almonds. Turn into medium saucepan; add 1/3 cup sugar, 1/2 cup water, 1 teaspoon lemon zest, and 2 tablespoons lemon juice. Cook over medium heat, stirring constantly, until mixture comes to a boil and is thickened (5 to 8 minutes). Cool completely before using.

Prune Bars: Follow directions for Fig Filling but substitute 2 cups lightly packed moist-pack pitted prunes for figs and add 3/4 teaspoon ground cinnamon with sugar.

Date Bars: Follow directions for Fig Filling but substitute 1 pound pitted dates for figs and increase lemon zest to 2 teaspoons.

Apricot Bars: Follow directions for Fig Filling but substitute 3 cups lightly packed dried apricots for figs and use 1 teaspoon orange zest instead of lemon zest.

Mango Bars: Use purchased or homemade Mango Chutney as filling.

Buttery Hawaiian Lemon Bars

Yield: About 24 bars

These luscious bars will remind you of Lemon
Meringue Pie with a cookie crust.

Crust:
1 cup butter or margarine, softened
$1/2$ cup powdered sugar
$2^{1}/_{4}$ cups flour

Filling:
4 eggs
2 cups sugar
1 teaspoons lemon zest
$1/2$ cup fresh lemon juice
$1/2$ cup flour
1 teaspoon baking powder
$1/4$ teaspoon salt
Powdered sugar

To prepare Crust, beat butter and powdered sugar together in large mixer bowl until creamy; beat in flour, blending thoroughly. Spread mixture evenly over bottom of well-greased 9 × 13 × 2-inch baking pan. Bake. Temperature: 350°F. Time: 18 to 20 minutes or until light golden brown.

Prepare Filling by beating eggs in small mixer bowl until light. Gradually add sugar, beating until mixture thickens and turns lemon-colored. Add lemon zest, lemon juice, flour, baking powder, and salt; beat until smooth and well combined. Pour Filling mixture over baked crust and return to oven; bake additional 15 to 20 minutes or until topping is light golden brown. Place on rack to cool; sprinkle with sifted powdered sugar while still warm over top. Cool. Cut into bars to serve. Store in airtight container.

Chocolate Coconut Bars

Yield: About 24 bars

The addition of coconut to this cookie adds a delightful mix of flavor with chocolate.

1 cup sugar
$1/2$ cup butter or margarine, softened
1 cup sweetened flaked or shredded coconut
2 eggs, slightly beaten
$1 1/2$ cups flour
1 tablespoon baking powder
1 teaspoon ground cinnamon
$1/2$ teaspoon salt
$1/4$ teaspoon nutmeg
1 cup semi-sweet chocolate pieces

Cream sugar and butter or margarine until light and fluffy. Stir in coconut and eggs; mix well. Add all dry ingredients that have been mixed together; blend into creamed mixture. Stir in chocolate pieces; mix well. Spread evenly into greased 9 × 13 × 2-inch baking pan. Bake. Temperature: 350°F. Time: 20 to 25 minutes. Cool. Cut into bars.

Macadamia Butter Bars

Yield: About 32 bars

The crunchy, exotic flavor of toasted macadamia nuts combined with butter makes these bar cookies almost irresistible.

- -

1 cup butter or margarine, softened
1 cup sugar
1 egg, slightly beaten
1 teaspoon vanilla extract
2 cups flour
1 1/4 cups macadamia nut bits

In large mixer bowl, cream butter or margarine and sugar until light and fluffy. Beat in egg and vanilla. Stir in flour and 1/2 cup of nuts. Spread batter evenly in greased 9 × 13 × 2-inch pan. Sprinkle remaining nuts over batter. Bake. Temperature: 350°F. Time: 25 to 30 minutes or until light golden brown. Cut into bars while hot and remove from pan while warm.

Guava Bars

Yield: About 24 bars

These exotic, fruity treats make an interesting and delicious addition to the cookie tray.

Crust:
1 cup flour
1 teaspoon baking soda
2¼ cups quick-cooking oatmeal
1 cup brown sugar, packed
1 cup butter or margarine, melted

Filling:
4 eggs, slightly beaten
1¼ cups sugar
½ cup frozen guava juice concentrate, thawed
½ teaspoon fresh lemon juice
½ cup flour
1 teaspoon baking powder
⅛ teaspoon salt
Powdered sugar

For Crust, mix together flour, baking soda, oatmeal, and brown sugar; add butter or margarine and toss to blend all ingredients thoroughly. Press mixture into lightly greased 9 × 13 × 2-inch pan, building up sides slightly. Bake. Temperature: 350°F. Time: 20 to 25 minutes. Set aside.

To prepare Filling, beat eggs; add sugar, guava juice, and lemon juice. Mix flour, baking powder, and salt together; add to liquid mixture. Pour Filling mixture over Crust and bake additional 25 to 30 minutes or until Filling is set. Cool. Sprinkle with powdered sugar. Cut into bars to serve.

Date Oatmeal Bars

Yield: About 24 bars

A healthy after-school snack for children, this bar cookie can be served as a simple dessert—especially one with a scoop of ice cream!

Filling:

2 cups chopped dates

$1/2$ cup brown sugar, packed

1 cup water

1 tablespoon flour

1 teaspoon vanilla extract

Dry Mixture:

$1 1/4$ cup flour

1 teaspoon baking soda

$2 1/4$ cups quick-cooking oatmeal

1 cup brown sugar, packed

1 cup butter or margarine, melted

Combine dates, brown sugar, water, and flour in a saucepan; bring to a boil over medium heat; reduce heat to low and simmer 3 to 5 minutes or until thickened. Add vanilla; stir and set aside.

Mix together flour, baking soda, oatmeal, brown sugar, and butter or margarine; blend ingredients thoroughly and divide mixture into two parts. Press one-half of dry mixture into greased 9-inch square cake pan. Pour cooled Filling over dry mixture layer; spread evenly. Sprinkle remaining dry mixture evenly over Filling. Bake. Temperature: 350°F. Time: 20 minutes or until light golden brown. Cool and cut into bars to serve.

Blondies

Yield: About 24 bars

These chewy bars are made with butter and brown sugar for a rich flavor and a handsome golden hue. Blondies are sometimes referred to as Butterscotch Brownies.

$1/4$ cup butter or margarine
1 cup brown sugar, packed
1 egg, slightly beaten
1 teaspoon vanilla extract
1 cup flour
1 teaspoon baking powder
$1/2$ teaspoon salt
$1/4$ cup chopped nuts

Melt butter or margarine in medium-size saucepan over medium heat. Remove from heat and stir in sugar, egg and vanilla; beat until well combined. Stir in flour, baking powder, salt, and nuts. Spread batter evenly in a greased 8-inch square baking pan. Bake. Temperature: 350°F. Time: 20 to 25 minutes or until golden brown. Do not overbake. Cool. Cut into bars. Store airtight. Sprinkle with powdered sugar just before serving, if desired.

Variations:

Chocolate Chip Blondies: Add 1 cup semi-sweet chocolate chips to dough. Proceed as directed.

Raisin Blondies: Substitute 1/4 cup raisins for nuts.

Mac Nut-Cheesecake Bars

Yield: About 24 bars

Delicious! These bars are packed with the rich flavors of cream cheese and macadamia nuts—certainly worth an afternoon break with milk, coffee, or tea.

1 cup flour
$1/_3$ cup butter or margarine, softened
$1/_3$ cup brown sugar, packed
$1/_2$ cup chopped macadamia nuts
1 egg, beaten
1 (8-ounce) package cream cheese, softened
$1/_4$ cup sugar
2 tablespoons milk
1 tablespoon lemon juice
$1/_2$ teaspoon vanilla extract

Fresh fruit slices of choice, optional

Combine flour, butter, and brown sugar in small mixer bowl; mix on low speed until mixture is mealy. Stir in nuts; set aside 1 cup for topping. Press remainder into ungreased 8-inch square pan. Bake. Temperature: 350°F. Time: 12 to 15 minutes or until light brown. Combine remaining ingredients in small mixer bowl; beat well on medium speed; pour over baked crust and spread evenly. Sprinkle with reserved flour mixture. Bake for additional 25 to 30 minutes. Cool; cut into bars. If desired, top with fresh fruit of choice to serve.

Left: Mac Nut-Cheesecake Bars
Right: Chocolate Kiss Brownies (see page 37)

Peanut Butter Brownies

Yield: About 12 bars

*Peanuts and chocolate is a tempting combination,
especially in these bar cookies.*

$^3/_4$ cup creamy peanut butter
$^1/_3$ cup butter or margarine, softened
$^3/_4$ cup brown sugar, packed
2 eggs
1 teaspoon vanilla extract
1 cup flour
1 teaspoon baking powder
$^1/_4$ teaspoon salt
$^1/_2$ cup semi-sweet chocolate pieces

Beat together peanut butter, butter or margarine, and sugar until light and fluffy. Add eggs, one at a time beating well after each addition; add vanilla and mix well. Stir in flour, baking powder, and salt that have been mixed together; add chocolate and mix well. Spread batter into greased 9 × 9-inch baking pan. Bake. Temperature: 350°F. Time: 20 to 25 minutes. Cool. Cut into bars. If desired, frost with icing of your choice.

Favorite Brownies

Yield: About 16 to 20 bars

I can't imagine a collection of recipes without one or more brownie recipes so here are some of my favorites.

1/3 cup butter or margarine
1 (1-ounce) square unsweetened chocolate
1 cup sugar
3/4 cup flour
1/2 teaspoon salt
1/2 teaspoon baking powder
2 eggs, slightly beaten
1 teaspoon vanilla extract
1 cup chopped nuts
Powdered sugar, optional

Melt butter or margarine and chocolate in 2-quart saucepan; remove from heat and stir in sugar. Sift together flour, salt, and baking powder; add to chocolate mixture. Beat in eggs. Stir in vanilla and nuts. Pour batter into greased 8- or 9-inch square cake pan. Bake. Temperature: 350°F. Time: 20 to 30 minutes. For extra chewy brownies use 8-inch pan and less baking time. For cakey brownies, use 9-inch pan and longer baking time. Cool and cut into bars. Sprinkle with powdered sugar, if desired.

Variations:
Chocolate Chip Brownies: Add 1 cup chocolate chips to Favorite Brownie batter. Proceed as directed above.
Chocolate Kisses Brownies: Cut brownies into approximately 1-1/2-inch squares and press an unwrapped chocolate kiss candy on top while warm. Yield: About 25.
Mac Nut Brownies: Add 1 cup chopped nuts to Favorite Brownie batter. Proceed as directed above.

Cream Cheese Brownies

Yield: About 24 bars

This is a delicious variation of the traditional brownie. It can be made in advance, covered, and refrigerated for up to 2 days.

1 recipe Favorite Brownies (see page 37)

1 (8-ounce) package cream cheese, softened
$1/3$ cup sugar
1 egg, slightly beaten
$1/2$ teaspoon vanilla extract

Prepare brownie as directed in Favorite Brownies recipe. To prepare the cheese mixture, mix together in a small mixer bowl the cream cheese with sugar until well blended. Stir in egg and vanilla; beat to blend thoroughly. Spread two-thirds of brownie batter evenly in greased 8- or 9-inch pan. Spread cream cheese mixture evenly over batter. Spoon remaining brownie batter in heaps over cream cheese mixture. Using a knife or skewer, cut through batter several times for marble effect. Bake. Temperature: 350°F. Time: 20 to 25 minutes or until just set in the center. Cool. Cut into squares.

Above: Triple Layered Brownies (see page 40)

Below: Cream Cheese Brownies

Triple-Layered Brownies

Yield: About 32 bars

These triple-layered treats have been favorites
since the days of the Beach Boys.

Bottom Layer

1 cup quick-cooking oatmeal

$1/2$ cup flour

$1/2$ cup brown sugar, packed

$1/4$ teaspoon baking soda

$1/2$ cup melted butter

Middle Layer

1 egg, slightly beaten

$3/4$ cup sugar

$2/3$ cup flour

$1/4$ cup milk

$1/4$ cup melted butter

1 ounce unsweetened chocolate, melted and cooled

1 teaspoon vanilla extract

1 teaspoon baking powder

$1/2$ cup chopped walnuts or pecans

Top Layer

1 (1-ounce) square unsweetened chocolate

2 tablespoons butter

$1 1/2$ cups sifted powdered sugar

$1/2$ teaspoon vanilla extract

Walnut or pecan halves, optional

For Bottom Layer, stir together oatmeal, flour, brown sugar, and baking soda. Stir in the melted butter. Press mixture into bottom of ungreased 11 × 7 × 1-1/2-inch pan. Bake. Temperature: 350°F. Time: 10 minutes.

Meanwhile, for Middle Layer, stir together egg, sugar, flour, milk, butter, melted chocolate, vanilla, and baking powder until smooth. Fold in chopped nuts. Spread batter over baked layer in pan. Return to oven. Bake. Time: 25 minutes more or until wooden pick inserted near center comes out clean. Place pan on wire rack to cool while preparing top layer.

For Top Layer, heat and stir chocolate and butter in medium saucepan until melted. Stir in powdered sugar and vanilla. Stir in enough hot water (1 to 2 tablespoons) to make a mixture that is almost pourable. Spread over brownies. If desired, garnish with nut halves. Cool in pan on wire rack. Cut into bars to serve.

DROP COOKIES

Did you know that the very first cookie invented was a drop cookie? A small spoonful of cake batter was baked before the entire cake so that the cook could judge the oven temperature along with the flavor and texture of the batter. The word "cookie" comes from the Dutch word "koekje" meaning "little cake."

Next to bar cookies and brownies, drop cookies are the easiest to bake. As the name implies, the dough is "dropped" by spoonfuls onto the baking sheets. Drop cookies such as Stephen's Favorite Oatmeal Cookies or Alissa's Chocolate Chip Cookies are simple, old-fashioned, traditional, and homey creations.

Today, drop cookies take on a variety of forms from simple mounds embellished with nuts, raisins, or chocolate to a more sophisticated form such as the Mac Nut Macaroons.

Tips for Drop Cookies

- Spoon dough onto baking sheet with a tableware spoon, not a measuring spoon, unless level teaspoon or tablespoon is specified.
- Push dough onto baking sheet with another spoon or small rubber spatula.
- Use a spring-handle ice cream scoop for making uniformly shaped cookies.
- Drop dough about 2 inches apart (or as directed in recipe) onto baking sheet.
- Cookies were overbaked if edges are dark and crusty, the baking sheet was too large for oven or a dark baking sheet was used. If center of cookie is doughy, it was underbaked.
- Excess spreading of the dough may be caused by dough being too warm, baking sheet being too hot, or the oven temperature being incorrect.
- Chill soft dough before dropping onto baking sheet; let baking sheet cool between bakings.
- Do not overmix dough in order to avoid tough texture.

Stephen's Favorite Oatmeal Cookies

Yield: About 5 dozen

There is nothing my grandson, Stephen, likes more than "plain old-fashioned" Oatmeal Cookies for an after-school snack or a dessert after a hearty dinner. Yummy! It's even better with raisins and nuts for a wholesome treat.

· ·

1 cup butter or vegetable shortening, softened
1 cup brown sugar, packed
$1/2$ cup sugar
1 egg
$1/4$ cup water
$3/4$ teaspoon vanilla extract
3 cups oatmeal (quick or old-fashioned, uncooked)
1 cup flour
1 teaspoon salt
$1/2$ teaspoon baking soda

Beat together butter or shortening, sugars, egg, water, and vanilla until creamy. Combine oats, flour, salt, and baking soda; stir into creamed mixture; mix well. Drop by rounded teaspoonfuls onto nonstick or ungreased cookie sheet. Bake. Temperature: 350°F. Time: 12 to 15 minutes or until light brown. Cool. These cookies keep well for a few weeks if stored in tightly covered container.

Variations:

• *Wholesome Oatmeal Cookies*: Add 1-1/2 cups of any combination of the following to Oatmeal Cookie dough: Raisins, chopped nuts, coconut, craisins, or chocolate chips. Proceed as above.

• *Oatmeal Raisin Cookies*: Add 1-1/2 cups of raisins to Oatmeal Cookie dough. Proceed as above.

• *Giant Oatmeal Cookies*: Drop dough by tablespoonfuls onto cookie sheet. Bake. Temperature: 375°F. Time: 12 to 15 minutes. Yield: About 2-1/2 dozen.

Toll Oats Cookies

Yield: About 3-1/2 dozen

A lunch box favorite! These chewy cookies pack well and the combination of rolled oats and chocolate is just perfect with cold milk. Oh, so 'ono!!!

• •

$1/2$ cup butter or margarine, softened
$1/2$ cup sugar
$1/2$ cup brown sugar, packed
1 egg, slightly beaten
1 tablespoon water
$1/2$ teaspoon vanilla extract
$13/4$ cups flour
$1/2$ teaspoon baking soda
$11/2$ cups quick-cooking oatmeal, uncooked
1 (6-ounce) package semi-sweet chocolate pieces

Cream butter or margarine with sugars until light and fluffy in medium mixer bowl. Add egg, water, and vanilla to creamed mixture; mix well. Sift together flour and baking soda; stir into creamed mixture and blend thoroughly. Add oatmeal, chocolate pieces, and nuts; stir to combine well. Drop by teaspoonfuls onto baking sheets. Bake. Temperature: 375°F. Time: 10 to 13 minutes. Do not overbake. Cool. Store in airtight container.

Basic Butter Cookies

Yield: About 4-1/2 to 5 dozen

*Here is a basic recipe from which a variety of
cookies can be made very simply.*

1 cup butter, softened
1$^1/_2$ cups sugar
1 egg, beaten
$^3/_4$ teaspoon vanilla extract
2$^1/_4$ cups flour
$^1/_2$ teaspoon baking soda
$^1/_2$ teaspoon salt

Cream butter and sugar until light and fluffy. Add egg and vanilla; mix well. Combine flour, baking soda and salt; mix well. Add to creamed mixture and mix thoroughly. Drop by teaspoonfuls, 1-1/2 to 2 inches apart, onto lightly greased cookie sheet. Bake. Temperature: 350°F. Time: 12 to 15 minutes. Cool. Store airtight.

Variations:

Chocolate Chips: Add 2 cups chocolate pieces to basic dough.

Cranberry Cookies: Add 2 cups dried cranberries or craisins to basic dough.

Nutty Cookies: Add 1-1/2 cups chopped nuts to basic dough.

Peanut Butter Cookies: Add 1 cup creamy or crunchy peanut butter to basic dough.

Raisin Cookies: Add 2 cups raisins to basic dough

Giant Cranberry Oatmeal Cookies

Yield: About 14

Perfect with a cup of full-flavored coffee! A super-size cookie with tart cranberries rather than traditional raisins.

· ·

$1/_2$ cup shortening, softened
$1/_2$ cup butter, softened
$3/_4$ cup brown sugar, packed
$1/_2$ cup sugar
1 teaspoon apple pie spice
$1/_2$ teaspoon baking powder
$1/_4$ teaspoon baking soda
$1/_4$ teaspoon salt
2 eggs, slightly beaten
1 teaspoon vanilla
$11/_3$ cups flour
$21/_2$ cups regular oatmeal, uncooked
1 cup dried cranberries
1 teaspoon orange zest

In large mixer bowl, beat shortening, butter, sugars, apple pie spice, baking powder, baking soda, and salt until light and fluffy. Add eggs and vanilla; beat thoroughly. Stir in flour, oatmeal, cranberries, and orange zest. Fill a 1/3-cup dry measure with dough and drop onto greased baking sheet. Press into 4-inch circle. Repeat with remaining dough, placing cookies 3 inches apart. Bake. Temperature: 375°F. Time: 8 to 10 minutes or until edges are golden. Let stand 1 minute on baking sheet; transfer to wire rack and cool completely. Store airtight.

Variation:
Oatmeal Cinnamon Cookies: Add 2 cups flour instead of 1-1/3 cups and 2 teaspoons ground cinnamon to dough, omit cranberries.

Alissa's Chocolate Chip Cookies

Yield: About 5 dozen

The original chocolate chip cookie, Toll House Cookie, got its name from a lovely old tollhouse owned by Mr. & Mrs. Wakefield who turned the historic old house into the now-famous Toll House Inn located between Boston and New Bedford, Massachusetts. Mrs. Wakefield first baked the original Toll House Cookies for guests at the Inn. Since then, there have been many variations. These are Alissa's favorite and she likes them right-out-of-the-oven!

1 cup butter or margarine, softened
$3/_4$ cup sugar
$3/_4$ cup light brown sugar, packed
2 eggs, beaten
1 teaspoon vanilla extract
$2^1/_4$ cups flour
1 teaspoon baking soda
1 teaspoon salt
2 cups (12 ounce package) semi-sweet chocolate chips

In a large mixing bowl, cream butter or margarine with sugars until light and fluffy. Add eggs and vanilla; beat well. Combine flour, baking soda, and salt; mix well and gradually mix into creamed mixture. Stir in chocolate chips. Drop by rounded tablespoon onto ungreased baking sheets. Bake. Temperature 375°F. Time: 9 to 11 minutes or until golden brown. Let stand 1 to 2 minutes; remove to wire racks to cool completely. Store in airtight container.

Variations:

Hawaiian Chocolate Chip: Add 1 cup chopped macadamia nuts and 1 cup shredded coconut to Chocolate Chip Cookie recipe. Yield: About 5-1/2 dozen.

Chocolate Chip Bars: Prepare dough as directed above; spread into 9 × 13 × 2-inch pan. Bake. Time: 20 to 25 minutes or until golden brown. Cool in pan; cut into bars. Yield: About 24 to 30 bars.

Drop Cookies

Krispy Krunchies
Yield: About 4 dozen

*Truly the cookie for chocolate lovers—these oversized
treats have a trio of chocolates!*

1 cup butter or margarine, softened
2 cups sugar
2 eggs
$1/_2$ cup chunky peanut butter
2 cups flour
1 teaspoon baking soda
1 teaspoon baking powder
2 teaspoons vanilla extract
1 cup quick oats
2 cups crisp rice cereal
1 (6-ounce) package chocolate pieces

Cream butter and sugar until light and fluffy. Add eggs, one at a time,
beating well after each addition. Add peanut butter and mix well. Gradually add flour, baking soda, and baking powder, which have been mixed
together; stir in remaining ingredients. Drop by rounded teaspoonfuls
onto lightly greased cookie sheets. Bake. Temperature: 350°F. Time: 15
to 20 minutes or until lightly brown.

Left: Krispy Krunchies
Above: Wholesome Oatmeal Cookies with cranberries (see page 45)

Rainbow Cookies
Yield: About 4 dozen

This recipe came from a good friend who bakes them year 'round to keep her cookie jar full and her grandchildren happy. These easy-to-bake cookies are crispy, colorful, and 'ono!

1 cup butter or margarine, softened
3/4 cup sugar
3/4 cup brown sugar, packed
3 1/2 cups flour
1 teaspoon salt
1 teaspoon baking soda
1 egg, slightly beaten
1 cup canola oil
1 teaspoon vanilla extract
1 cup quick-cooking oatmeal
1 cup cornflakes or raisin bran
1 cup chopped nuts
1/2 cup sweetened shredded coconut
1 cup semi-sweet chocolate chips
1 cup miniature candy-coated chocolate pieces
1/2 cup raisins, optional

Cream butter or margarine with sugars until light and fluffy. Sift together flour, salt, and baking soda; stir into creamed mixture. Add remaining ingredients; mix well and drop by heaping teaspoonfuls onto ungreased baking sheets. Bake. Temperature: 350°F. Time: 15 minutes or until light brown. Cool. Store in airtight container.

Chocolate Puffs

Yield: About 3 dozen

You'll enjoy the mixture of coconut, macadamia nuts, and chocolate in this macaroon-type cookie. This cookie is best if made just before serving as it doesn't store well for long.

2 egg whites
$^1/_2$ cup sugar
$^1/_4$ teaspoon salt
1 teaspoon vanilla extract
1 (6-ounce) package semi-sweet chocolate pieces, melted
$1^1/_4$ cups fresh or frozen shredded coconut
$^1/_2$ cup chopped macadamia nuts

Whisk egg whites in a large, clean, grease-free bowl until stiff peaks form. Gradually whisk in sugar until blended. Add salt and vanilla; fold in melted chocolate, coconut, and nuts. Drop by teaspoonfuls onto baking sheet. Bake. Temperature: 300°F. Time: 10 to 15 minutes or until set. Cool on baking sheets for a few minutes before transferring to wire rack to cool completely. Store in airtight container using wax paper between layers if stacking.

Mac Nut Macaroons
Yield: About 36

This recipe is a variation of Hickory Nut Macaroons, which was first published around eighty years ago. It still continues to be one of the best-loved cookies.

4 egg whites
4 cups sifted powdered sugar
2 cups macadamia nut bits

Beat egg white in a large mixing bowl on high speed until stiff peaks form. Gradually add powdered sugar, about 2 to 4 tablespoons at a time, beating at medium speed just until combined; beat additional 1 to 2 minutes or until combined. Fold in nuts and drop mixture by rounded teaspoons 2 inches apart on greased baking sheet. Bake. Temperature: 325°F. Time: 15 minutes or until edges are very lightly browned. Transfer cookies to a wire rack and cool completely. Store in airtight container using wax paper between layers.

Note:
If desired, see directions for Coconut Macaroons and bake on parchment paper. Continue as directed in Coconut Macaroons recipe (see page 59).

Coconut Macaroons

Yield: About 2-1/2 dozen

Macaroons are classic no-fuss cookies. They are easy to whisk up in minutes and always appreciated. The coconut makes this recipe excitingly different.

• •

$^1/_2$ cup egg whites
$1^1/_4$ cups sugar
$^1/_4$ teaspoon salt
$^1/_2$ teaspoon vanilla extract
$2^1/_2$ cups fresh or frozen shredded coconut

Whisk egg white until fluffy; stir in sugar, salt, and vanilla; mix well. Blend in coconut. Drop by rounded teaspoonfuls 2 inches apart on parchment paper lined baking sheet. Bake. Temperature: 325°F. Time: 15 to 18 minutes or until set and delicately browned. They spread during baking so when they come from the oven, shape into mounds by gathering in edges with fingers. Remove paper from baking sheet with baked macaroons on it. Lay a wet towel on the hot baking sheet; place paper of Macaroons on towel and let stand 1 minute. Steam will loosen Macaroons. Slip macaroons off with spatula. Cool. Store in airtight container with wax paper between layers if stacked.

Above: Chocolate Puffs (see page 56)

Left: Coconut Macaroons

Right: Mac Nut Macaroons (see page 57)

Macadamia Clusters

Yield: About 3 dozen

These crispy cookies are deliciously nutty. They are great for snacks and especially good to keep the cookie jar filled.

• •

$1/_4$ cup butter or margarine

$1/_2$ cup sugar

1 egg, slightly beaten

$1 1/_2$ teaspoons vanilla extract

$1 1/_2$ (1-ounce) squares unsweetened chocolate, melted

$1/_2$ cup flour

$1/_4$ teaspoon baking powder

$1/_2$ teaspoon salt

2 cups coarsely chopped macadamia nuts

Cream together butter or margarine and sugar until light and fluffy. Add egg and vanilla; mix well. Mix in melted chocolate, then the dry ingredients, which have been sifted together. Stir in the nuts; mix well. Drop 1 inch apart by teaspoonfuls onto a baking sheet. Bake. Temperature: 350°F. Time: 10 minutes. Be careful not to burn cookies.

Giant Triple Chocolate Cookies

Yield: About 22

*Truly the cookie for chocolate lovers—these oversized
treats have a trio of chocolates!*

1 cup butter or margarine, softened
$3/_4$ cup sugar
$3/_4$ cup brown sugar, packed
1 teaspoon baking soda
2 eggs, slightly beaten
$3/_4$ teaspoon vanilla extract
3 (1-ounce) squares unsweetened chocolate, melted and cooled
2 cups flour
$1^1/_3$ cups semisweet chocolate pieces
1 cup white baking pieces
1 cup chopped nuts, optional

Beat butter or margarine until light and fluffy in large mixer bowl. Beat
in sugars and baking soda until well combined. Beat in eggs and vanilla
until combined. Stir in melted chocolate, flour, chocolate pieces, white
baking pieces, and if desired, nuts. Using 1/4-cup dry measure or scoop,
drop mounds of dough about 4 inches apart on lightly greased baking
sheet. Bake. Temperature: 350°F. Time: 12 to 14 minutes or until edges
are firm. Cool on baking sheet 1 minute; transfer to wire rack; cool completely. Store in airtight container.

Macadamia Lace Cookies

Yield: About 50

These delicate cookies are intensely flavored with rich macadamia nuts and deeply browned butter.

. . . .

$^1/_2$ cup unsalted butter, cut into 5 pieces
1 cup finely chopped, lightly salted macadamia nuts
1 cup sugar
1 egg, slightly beaten
1 teaspoon vanilla extract
$^1/_4$ teaspoon salt

Melt butter in small saucepan over medium heat until butter solids at the bottom of the pan turn deep golden brown (5 to 7 minutes), not black. Watch the butter carefully. Remove pan from heat immediately and put butter into small bowl, scraping pan to get all the butter. Let cool about 5 minutes.

Combine macadamia nuts, sugar, egg, vanilla, and salt in medium bowl; stir until blended. Slowly add browned butter and continue stirring until well blended. Drop batter by teaspoonfuls about 3 inches apart on baking sheets lined with parchment paper or nonstick baking liners. Bake. Temperature: 350°F. Time: 6 to 8 minutes or until golden brown. Cool cookies on the baking sheet on racks for 5 minutes; transfer to racks to cool completely. Repeat with remaining batter after the sheets have cooled. Store or freeze in airtight container, separating cookie layers with wax paper.

Variation:
Chocolate Macadamia Lace Cookies: Coat bottoms of cookies with melted chocolate; set aside to cool.

Coconut Island Cookies
Yield: About 3 dozen

A one-time cookie contest winner, this cookie may take a little time to pre-pare but it is certainly worth the effort, especially if you are a "chocoholic."

$\cdot$ $\cdot$ $\cdot$ $\cdot$ $\cdot$ $\cdot$ $\cdot$ $\cdot$ $\cdot$ $\cdot$ $\cdot$ $\cdot$ $\cdot$ $\cdot$ $\cdot$ $\cdot$ $\cdot$ $\cdot$ $\cdot$ $\cdot$ $\cdot$ $\cdot$ $\cdot$ $\cdot$ $\cdot$ $\cdot$ $\cdot$ $\cdot$ $\cdot$ $\cdot$ $\cdot$ $\cdot$ $\cdot$ $\cdot$ $\cdot$ $\cdot$ $\cdot$ $\cdot$ $\cdot$

$1/_2$ cup butter or margarine, softened
1 cup brown sugar, packed
3 (1-ounce) squares unsweetened chocolate, melted
$1/_4$ cup strong brewed coffee
1 egg, slightly beaten
2 cups flour
$1/_4$ teaspoon salt
$1/_2$ teaspoon baking soda
$1/_2$ cup sour milk
$1/_2$ cup fresh or frozen grated coconut

Icing:
2 (1-ounce) squares unsweetened chocolate
1 tablespoon butter or margarine
1 cup powdered sugar, sifted
2 tablespoons sour milk
$1/_3$ cup fresh or frozen grated coconut

Cream together butter or margarine and brown sugar in small mixer bowl until light and fluffy. Add melted chocolate, coffee, and egg; beat well. Stir flour, salt, and baking soda together. Add alternately to creamed mixture with sour milk, beginning and ending with flour mixture. Fold in grated coconut. Drop by teaspoonfuls onto baking sheet. Bake. Temperature: 350°F. Time: 10 to 12 minutes. Set aside.

To prepare Icing, melt chocolate and butter or margarine together. Add powdered sugar slowly with sour milk; mix until Icing is of spreading consistency. Drop a teaspoon of Icing onto each warm cookie and sprinkle with additional coconut.

PRESSED & SHAPED COOKIES

Pressed and shaped cookies are your fancy cookies for the simple fact that there are endless things you can do with the pliable dough they're made from. They can be rolled in sugar, nuts, or coconut; filled with jam, jelly, or chutney; flattened with a fork in a crisscross pattern or with a glass dipped in flour. You can even form them into a variety of shapes: balls, pretzels, crescents, and more.

Pressed and shaped cookies are often time-consuming to make since they are individually crafted, but they're worth the effort. Cookies can also be shaped with a cookie press. Pushing soft dough through a cookie press or pastry bag will create treats such as Spritz.

Making pressed and shaped cookies is a labor of love.

Tips for Pressed & Shaped Cookies

- Read through a recipe before beginning.
- Pressed and shaped cookies often take longer to make. For best results, make sure cookies are the same size and shape.
- Use room temperature butter, margarine, or shortening.
- Chill dough only if specified in the recipe.
- Baking sheet should always be cool before placing dough.
- When using a cookie press, hold it so it rests on the baking sheet. Raise the press straight up from the cookie sheet after dough has been released to form cookie.
- Dough should be soft and pliable but not crumbly. If dough is too stiff for cookie press, add 1 egg yolk; if dough is too soft, add 1 to 2 tablespoons flour.

Spritz

Yield: About 5 dozen

Ahh, Spritz Cookies—a cookie that evokes wonderful memories of my youth. Spritzing the cookie dough out of the cookie press to form many fancy shapes gave me many hours of baking pleasure.

· ·

³/₄ cup butter or margarine, softened
¹/₂ cup sugar
1 egg yolk
¹/₄ teaspoon salt
1 teaspoon vanilla extract
2 cups flour, sifted
Colored sugars or decorettes

Cream butter or margarine and sugar until light and fluffy. Add egg yolk and beat well. Add salt, vanilla, and flour; mix until combined. Press through pastry tube or cookie press onto ungreased baking sheets. Decorate with colored sugars or decorettes, if desired. Bake. Temperature: 425°F. Time: 8 to 10 minutes or until golden brown. Cool and store in airtight container.

Pressed & Shaped Cookies

Cream Cheese Spritz

Yield: About 8 dozen

Baking dozens of pretty little cookies is a snap with today's easy-to-use cookie presses. These slightly tangy cookies date back to about forty years when Spritz cookies were very popular.

• •

1 cup unsalted butter, softened
1 (3-ounce) package cream cheese, softened
1 cup sugar
1 large egg, separated
1 teaspoon vanilla extract
2$\frac{1}{2}$ cups flour
Colored sugars or decorettes, optional

Beat the butter, cream cheese, and sugar together until light and fluffy, about 4 minutes. Add egg yolk and vanilla; beat until well blended. Stir in flour and mix until blended. Fit cookie press with desired die plate. Scoop about one-fourth of the dough into the barrel of the cookie press; spritz the cookies directly onto ungreased baking sheets about 1 inch apart. Brush tops with beaten egg white and sprinkle with colored sugars or decorettes of choice. Repeat with remaining dough. Bake: Temperature: 375°F. Time: 10 to 12 minutes or just golden around the edges. It's best to bake one sheet at a time. Cool cookies on baking sheet 5 minutes before transferring to rack to cool completely. Spritz more on cooled baking sheet. Store at room temperature or freeze in airtight container, separating the layers with wax paper.

Pressed & Shaped Cookies

Russian Tea Cookies

Yield: About 6 dozen

These were often baked to serve at receptions or teas during my college days. They're tasty and delicate—a real tea time treat.

• •

1 cup butter, softened
1/2 cup sugar
2 teaspoons vanilla extract
2 cups flour, sifted
1/2 teaspoon salt
2 cups finely chopped nuts (macadamia, pecans, walnuts)
Powdered sugar

Cream together butter, sugar, and vanilla until fluffy. Mix together flour and salt; add to the creamed mixture, blending thoroughly. Add nuts and mix well. Shape into 1-inch balls and place on baking sheets lined with parchment paper. Bake. Temperature: 325°F. Time: 15 to 20 minutes or until set. Do not brown. Cool; then roll in powdered sugar. Store in airtight container.

Pressed & Shaped Cookies

Oatmeal Crunchies

Yield: About 5 dozen

Mmm…what a wholesome treat these cookies are! They're especially good with a glass of cold milk or a cup of good coffee.

. . . .

$2^1/_4$ cups all-purpose flour
1 teaspoon baking soda
1 teaspoon baking powder
$^1/_2$ cup shortening
$^1/_2$ cup butter or margarine, softened
1 tablespoon peanut butter, optional
$^3/_4$ cup brown sugar, packed
$^3/_4$ cup sugar
2 eggs, beaten
1 teaspoon vanilla extract
2 cups quick-cooking oatmeal
2 cups toasted rice cereal
$^1/_2$ cup chopped macadamia nuts, optional

Mix together flour, baking soda, and baking powder; set aside. Cream together shortening, butter or margarine, peanut butter, and sugars until light and fluffy. Add eggs, one at a time, mixing well after each addition. Add vanilla and dry ingredients; mix just until moistened. Stir in cereals and nuts. Form into walnut-size balls and drop onto lightly greased baking sheets; press tops with bottom of glass dipped in flour to flatten slightly. Bake. Temperature: 350°F. Time: 20 minutes or until lightly browned. Cool and store in airtight container.

Pressed & Shaped Cookies

Cocoa Kisses

Especially for chocoholics who will love the surprise in the center.

. . . .

1 cup butter, softened
$^2/_3$ cup sugar
1 teaspoon vanilla extract
1$^3/_4$ cups flour
$^1/_4$ cup cocoa
$^1/_2$ cup chopped nuts
1 (9-ounce) package chocolate kisses, unwrapped
Powdered sugar, optional

Cream butter and sugar together; stir in vanilla. Stir in flour and cocoa; mix well. Stir in nuts; mix well. Wrap a tablespoon of dough around chocolate and roll to form ball. Place on ungreased baking sheet. Bake. Temperature: 325°F. Time: 10 to 12 minutes or until light brown. Cool. Roll in powdered sugar, if desired. Store airtight, separating the layers with wax paper.

Shortbread Cookies

These traditional cookies are always a hit with everyone. Its buttery flavor and melt-in-the-mouth texture are hard to resist. These were probably the first cookies that I learned to bake.

2 cups butter or margarine, softened
1 cup sugar
4 cups flour
2 teaspoons vanilla extract

Cream butter or margarine and sugar until light and fluffy. Stir in flour and vanilla; mix well. Either use dough immediately by putting it through a cookie press onto ungreased baking sheets 2 inches apart or shape dough into 2 rolls, about 2 inches in diameter; wrap in wax paper; chill several hours or overnight. Slice dough into 1/4-inch slices with a sharp knife; place 2 inches apart on ungreased baking sheets. Bake. Temperature: 325°F. Time: 20 to 25 minutes or until light golden brown. Cool. Store in airtight container.

Sesame Seed Cookies

Yield: About 10 dozen

*Bite into the flavor of toasted sesame seeds. These savory
cookies will keep your cookie jar filled!*

. . . .

1 cup butter or margarine, softened
1 cup sugar
1 egg, slightly beaten
1 teaspoon vanilla extract
2 cups flour
$1/2$ teaspoon baking soda
$1/4$ teaspoon salt
1 cup toasted sesame seeds

In a large mixer bowl cream together butter or margarine and sugar;
mix in egg and vanilla. Sift together flour, baking soda, and salt; stir into
creamed mixture. Chill about 1 hour. Shape dough into small balls then
roll in sesame seeds. Place on greased baking sheets and flatten with
the bottom of a glass dipped in flour. Bake. Temperature: 375°F. Time: 10
to 12 minutes or until golden brown. Cool. Store in airtight container.

Turtle Cookies

This variation of a favorite candy is made of pecans and a delicious cookie that's topped with a simple chocolate frosting.

. . . .

$1/_2$ cup butter or margarine, softened
$1/_2$ cup brown sugar, packed
1 egg, separated
$1/_4$ teaspoon vanilla extract
$1 1/_2$ cups flour
$1/_4$ teaspoon baking soda
$1/_4$ teaspoon salt
1 (6-ounce) can pecan halves

Chocolate Frosting:
2 (1-ounce) squares unsweetened chocolate
$1/_4$ cup milk
1 tablespoon butter
1 cup powdered sugar

Cream butter or margarine and sugar until light and fluffy; beat in egg yolk and vanilla. Gradually add flour, baking soda, and salt, which have been mixed together; mix well. Split pecan halves; arrange in groups of five on greased baking sheets for "head" and "legs" of turtle. Mold rounded teaspoons of dough into balls; dip bottoms into beaten egg white; press lightly onto pecans. Bake. Temperature: 350°F. Time: 10 to 12 minutes or until set. Cool. Frost tops with Chocolate Frosting.

To prepare Chocolate Frosting, combine chocolate, milk, and butter in saucepan; cook over low heat until chocolate melts. Remove from heat; add powdered sugar and beat until smooth and of desired consistency.

Chocolate Crinkles

Yield: About 6 dozen

The tops of these cookies puff up and crack, making an attractive dark and white contrast…an interesting addition to the cookie tray year-round.

2 cups sugar
$1/_2$ cup canola oil
2 teaspoons vanilla extract
4 (1-ounce) squares unsweetened baking chocolate, melted and cooled
4 large eggs
2 cups flour
2 teaspoons baking powder
$1/_2$ teaspoon salt
$1/_2$ cup powdered sugar, sifted

Mix together sugar, oil, vanilla, and chocolate in large bowl. Mix in eggs, one at a time, beating well after each addition. Stir in flour, baking powder, and salt; mix well. Cover and refrigerate, at least 2 to 3 hours. Roll chilled dough into 1-inch balls; roll in powdered sugar. Place about 2 inches apart on lightly greased baking sheet. Bake. Temperature: 350°F. Time: 10 to 12 minutes, or until no indentation remains when touched. Cool. If desired, sprinkle with additional powdered sugar when cooled.

Pressed & Shaped Cookies

Cornflake Cookies

*These cookies are very easy to make and my grandchildren
love to help me bake them. They especially love to roll the dough
in the crispy cereal before baking.*

- -

1 cup butter or margarine, softened
³/₄ cup sugar
2 teaspoons vanilla extract
2 cups flour
3 cups (or more) cornflakes

Cream butter or margarine with sugar until light and fluffy; gradually add vanilla and flour; mix well. Form dough into large marble-size pieces and roll in bowl of crushed cornflakes. Place on ungreased baking sheets; flatten slightly using the bottom of a glass dipped in flour. Bake. Temperature: 350°F. Time: 10 to 15 minutes until golden yellow but not brown. Cool. Store in airtight container.

Variations:

Macadamia Nut Cookies: Stir in 1/2 cup chopped macadamia nuts to dough. Bake as directed until golden brown.

Chinese Almond Cookies

Yield: About 6 dozen

These cookies have the most wonderful texture and flavor in one bite. They are the perfect ending to a Chinese meal, especially when served with a fragrant Chinese tea.

3 cups flour
1 cup sugar
$^1/_2$ teaspoon baking soda
$^1/_2$ teaspoon salt
1$^1/_2$ cups shortening
1 egg, beaten
2 teaspoons almond extract
Red food color

Sift flour, sugar, baking soda, and salt into large bowl. Cut in shortening until mixture resembles cornmeal. Combine egg with almond extract; stir into flour mixture, mixing well and kneading gently for 30 seconds. Form into walnut size-balls. Place on ungreased baking sheets. Dip chopstick in red food color and make a depression in center of each cookie. Bake. Temperature: 350°F. Time: 15 to 18 minutes. Cool. Store in tightly covered container.

Pressed & Shaped Cookies

Right: Chinese Almond Cookies

Left: Fortune Cookies (see page 82)

Fortune Cookies

Yield: About 2-1/2 dozen

*Did you know that Fortune Cookies are really not Chinese at all?
They are the innovation of a Los Angeles baker in the 1920s. They taste
good and they have always been popular with Chinese food.*

. . . .

1 cup flour

2 tablespoons cornstarch

$1/_2$ cup sugar

$1/_4$ teaspoon salt

$1/_2$ cup canola oil

$1/_2$ cup egg whites (whites of about 4 large eggs)

1 tablespoon water

2 teaspoons vanilla extract

Print fortunes, allowing a 1/2 × 3-inch area of paper for each; cut into strips, separating individual fortunes; place near oven. Also have saucepan or straight-sided bowl ready for shaping and muffin pan for cooling the cookies. In a bowl, stir together flour, cornstarch, sugar, and salt. Add oil and egg whites; beat until smooth. Beat in water and vanilla.

Drop batter by tablespoonfuls onto well-greased baking sheets and spread out evenly with back of spoon into 4-inch circles. (Bake only 1 or 2 cookies per sheet at first then increase to 4 per sheet as your shaping improves.) Bake. Temperature 300°F. Time: 13 to 14 minutes or until light golden brown. If underbaked, cookies will tear during shaping.

Working quickly, 1) remove one cookie at a time from oven using wide spatula and flip it over into gloved hand; 2) hold printed fortune strip in center of cookie while folding it in half; 3) grasp ends of cookie and draw gently down over edge of a pan or bowl to crease; 4) to ensure that cookies hold their shape as they cool, place them, ends down, in muffin pans. Repeat for remaining batter, using a cold, well-greased baking sheet for each batch. Store in airtight container after cooling.

Coconut Crisps

Yield: About 4 dozen

An old-time favorite with delicious cinnamon-sugar coating sprinkled on top…good especially with cold milk or hot tea.

- -

1 cup butter or margarine, softened
1 cup sugar
1 teaspoon vanilla extract
2 cups flour
1$\frac{1}{4}$ cups shredded coconut

Cream butter or margarine and sugar until light and fluffy. Add vanilla; beat thoroughly. Mix in flour then add coconut; mix well. Form into walnut-size balls and place on ungreased baking sheets and flatten with bottom of a glass dipped in flour. Bake. Temperature: 300°F. Time: 20 to 25 minutes or until golden brown. Cool; store in airtight container.

Old-Fashioned Peanut Butter Cookies

Yield: About 4 dozen

These cookies are definitely one of my favorites. For extra crunch, use chunky peanut butter.

• •

1 cup shortening
1 cup sugar
1 cup brown sugar, packed
1 teaspoon vanilla extract
2 eggs, slightly beaten
1½ cups peanut butter (creamy or crunchy)
3 cups flour
2 teaspoons baking powder
¼ teaspoon salt

Cream shortening with sugars and vanilla until light and fluffy. Add eggs; beat thoroughly. Stir in peanut butter. Combine flour, baking powder, and salt; mix well and stir into creamed mixture. Form into walnut-size balls; place on ungreased baking sheets. Press with back of fork to make a crisscross design. Bake. Temperature: 375°F. Time: 10 to 15 minutes or until light brown. Cool and store in airtight container.

Variation:

Peanut Butter and Jelly Cookies: Spoon your favorite jam onto one cookie and top with a second cookie.

Left: Peanut Blossom Cookies (page 86)
Right: Old Fashioned Peanut Butter Cookies

Peanut Blossom Cookies

Yield: About 2-1/2 dozen

These delicious nutty cookies are easy to make and topped with chocolate candy.

. . . .

$1/_2$ cup shortening
$1/_2$ cup chunky peanut butter
$1/_2$ cup sugar
$1/_2$ cup brown sugar, packed
1 egg, slightly beaten
1 teaspoon vanilla extract
$1 1/_3$ cups flour
1 teaspoon baking soda
$1/_2$ teaspoon salt
$1/_4$ cup sugar
$2 1/_2$ to 3 dozen miniature chocolate candy pieces, unwrapped

Beat shortening, peanut butter, brown sugar, and 1/2 cup granulated sugar in large mixing bowl until light and fluffy; beat in egg and vanilla. In another bowl, stir together flour, baking soda, and salt; gradually add to shortening mixture blending thoroughly. Place remaining 1/4 cup sugar in small bowl. Roll dough into 1-inch balls then roll in sugar to coat; place balls 2 inches apart on greased baking sheets. Bake. Temperature: 350°F. Time: 10 minutes. Remove cookies from oven and quickly top each cookie with an unwrapped chocolate candy piece; press down until cookie cracks around edges. Return to oven and bake additional 3 to 5 minutes or until light brown and firm to the touch. Cool and store in airtight containers.

Pressed & Shaped Cookies

Soft Ginger Cookies

Yield: About 24

Try it, you'll like it!

. . . .

2$^1/_4$ cups flour
2 teaspoons ground ginger
1 teaspoon baking soda
$^3/_4$ teaspoon ground cinnamon
$^1/_4$ teaspoon ground cloves
$^3/_4$ cup butter, softened
1 cup sugar
1 egg, slightly beaten
$^1/_4$ cup molasses
2 tablespoons sugar

Combine flour, ginger, baking soda, cinnamon, and cloves in a medium mixing bowl; set aside. In a large mixer bowl, beat butter for about 30 seconds on medium speed. Beat in the 1 cup sugar; add egg and molasses; beat well. Stir in flour mixture into egg mixture. Shape dough into 1-1/2-inch balls, using 1 heaping tablespoon dough for each. Roll balls in the 2 tablespoons sugar to coat; place on ungreased baking sheet about 2-1/2 inches apart. Bake. Temperature: 350°F. Time: 8 to 10 minutes or until light brown and puffy. Do not overbake. Cool cookies on baking sheet for 1 to 2 minutes; transfer to wire rack and cool completely. Store airtight.

Tropical Thumbprint Cookies

Yield: About 4 dozen

*A sweet "jewel" of tropical jam glistens in the center
of each of these nutty morsels.*

. . . .

1 cup butter, softened
1 cup sugar
2 teaspoons vanilla extract
2 eggs, separated
2$^1/_2$ cups flour, sifted
1 cup finely chopped nuts (macadamia, pecans, walnuts)
Guava or poha jam

Beat the butter, sugar, vanilla, and egg yolks together in a medium-size bowl until light and fluffy. Gradually stir in the flour. Gather the dough in a ball, wrap in plastic and refrigerate until firm, about 4 hours. Form dough into balls by using a level teaspoon. Dip the balls in the egg white then roll in chopped nuts; place on ungreased baking sheets, approximately 1 inch apart. Make an indentation in each cookie with thumb or end of a wooden spoon; fill with jam. Bake. Temperature: 300°F. Time: 20 minutes or until golden. Cool. Store in airtight containers with wax paper between layers if they are stacked.

Variations:
Christmas Wreaths: Fill indentations with strawberry jam or mint jelly.
Jam Thumbprints: Fill indentations with cherry or apricot jam or preserves.

Snickerdoodles
Yield: About 4 dozen

An old-time favorite with delicious cinnamon-sugar coating sprinkled on top…good especially with cold milk or hot tea.

• •

1 cup butter or margarine, softened
$1^1/_2$ cups sugar
2 eggs, beaten
1 teaspoon vanilla extract
$2^3/_4$ cups flour
2 teaspoons baking powder
$^1/_2$ teaspoon salt

2 teaspoons cinnamon
3 tablespoons sugar

Cream butter or margarine with sugar until light and fluffy. Add eggs and vanilla; beat well. Mix together flour, baking powder, and salt; add to creamed mixture and mix thoroughly. Chill dough 1 hour. Form dough into walnut-size balls. In small bowl, mix together cinnamon and sugar; roll dough in mixture to coat. Place 2 inches apart on lightly greased baking sheets. Bake. Temperature: 375°F. Time: 10 to 12 minutes or until golden brown. Cool completely and store in airtight container.

Potato Chip Cookies

Yield: About 30

Adding potato chips to a cookie dough results in a new, delicious, crunchy, buttery cookie. Do not refrigerate or freeze the unbaked dough, however, as the potato chips will become soggy.

1 cup unsalted butter, softened
$1/2$ cup sugar
1 teaspoon vanilla extract
2 cups flour
$1/2$ cup chopped macadamia nuts
$1/2$ cup finely crushed potato chips

Beat the butter and sugar until light and fluffy in a medium mixer bowl using medium speed, about 3 to 4 minutes. Add vanilla; beat until blended. Add the flour, nuts, and potato chips; mix until all ingredients are blended. Shape into 1-inch balls; arrange 2 inches apart on parchment lined baking sheets. Press down, using bottom of glass dipped in sugar, until balls are about 1/4-inch thick. Bake. Temperature: 350°F. Time: 10 to 12 minutes. Cool cookies on the sheets on racks 5 minutes before transferring cookies to racks to cool completely. Store in airtight containers, separating cookie layers with wax paper.

Biscotti Toscani

Yield: About 3-1/2 dozen

Biscotti is the plural of "biscotto," or biscuit and refers to all kinds of cookies—not just the crunchy, twice-baked variety we often refer to.

· ·

$1/_3$ cup butter, softened
$3/_4$ cup sugar
2 eggs, slightly beaten
1 teaspoon vanilla extract
$1/_2$ teaspoon almond extract
2 teaspoons orange zest
$2^1/_4$ cups flour
$1^1/_2$ teaspoons baking powder
$1/_4$ teaspoon salt
$1/_4$ teaspoon ground cinnamon
$1/_2$ cup chopped almonds or hazelnut

In a mixing bowl, cream butter and sugar together until light and fluffy. Beat in eggs, vanilla and almond extracts, and orange zest. In another bowl, combine flour, baking powder, salt, and cinnamon; add to creamed mixture, mixing until well blended. Fold in nuts.

Divide dough in half and shape into two 11-inch logs. Place about 5 inches apart on lightly greased baking sheet. Flatten logs slightly until about 2 inches wide. Bake. Temperature: 325°F. Time: 20 to 25 minutes or until light brown. Cool logs on baking sheet on wire rack for about 20 minutes. Place logs on cutting board and cut each log diagonally into 1/2-inch slices with serrated knife. Lay slices, cut side down, on un-greased baking sheet; return to oven. Bake 10 minutes. Turn slices over; bake additional 10 to 15 minutes or until dry and crisp. Cool completely on wire rack. Store in airtight container until ready to serve.

SLICE & BAKE COOKIES

Slice and bake cookies were called "icebox" or "refrigerator" cookies when I was growing up. They are the quickest way to fill the cookie jar and to make fabulous cookies for sharing with friends and family.

These cookies offer make-ahead ease and adaptability, allowing no excuses even for bakers whose time is limited. They are made by forming the dough into long logs, refrigerating it until firm and then slicing it crosswise into ready-to-bake cookies. The dough can be prepared days or even weeks in advance in the freezer. Slicing and baking also can be done at your convenience.

These cookies are generally uniform, wafer-like with a crisp texture. If you want cookies with decorated edges, just roll the log of dough in sugar or nuts just before chilling. You can also create fancy treats such as pinwheels. The variations are unlimited.

Tips for Slice & Bake Cookies

Shape refrigerator cookie dough firmly into a small roll of the length or diameter specified in recipe. Wrap rolled dough in wax paper, plastic wrap, or aluminum foil, twisting ends.

- Refrigerate rolled dough until it is firm enough to slice easily, usually for several hours to overnight.
- Use a thin, sharp knife to slice dough.
- To keep cookies round while cutting the dough, rotate the roll frequently while slicing.
- Rolls of dough can be refrigerated up to 24 hours or wrapped airtight and frozen up to 12 months.

Gingerbread Cookies

Yield: About 7 dozen

*These are a supreme treat for ginger lovers—richly spiced
cookies that will give you a boost of energy.*

• •

1 cup butter or margarine
1 1/2 cups dark brown sugar, packed
2 eggs, slightly beaten
1/2 cup dark molasses
5 cups flour
1 tablespoon baking powder
1 1/2 teaspoons ground ginger
1 1/2 teaspoons ground cinnamon
1 teaspoon ground cloves
1/2 teaspoon salt

In large mixer bowl, cream butter or margarine and sugar. Add eggs
and molasses; beat well. Sift remaining ingredients together and add to
creamed mixture; mix well. Chill dough for several hours or overnight.
Using a sharp knife, cut into 1/4-inch slices on lightly floured board.
Place 1 inch apart on ungreased baking sheets. Bake. Temperature:
350°F. Time: 10 to 12 minutes or until light brown. Cool. Store in airtight
container until ready to decorate or serve.

Lemon Refrigerator Cookies

Yield: About 6-1/2 dozen

*Perfect for when you crave something sweet but
don't want the richness of chocolate.*

• •

1 cup butter or margarine, softened
$1/2$ cup sugar
$1/2$ cup brown sugar, packed
3 tablespoons fresh lemon juice
1 egg, slightly beaten
4 cups flour
$1/4$ teaspoon baking soda
1 tablespoon lemon zest
$1/2$ cup finely chopped macadamia nuts

Cream together butter or margarine with sugars. Add lemon juice and
egg; beat well. Sift together flour and baking soda and add to creamed
mixture. Add lemon zest and nuts; mix until well blended. Shape into 4
rolls, 2 inches in diameter; wrap each roll in wax paper. Chill until firm for
several hours or overnight. Cut chilled rolls into 1/8-inch slices; place on
ungreased baking sheet. Decorate with colored sprinkles or other decorations. Bake. Temperature: 400°F. Time: 9 minutes or until light brown.

Cinnamon Refrigerator Cookies

Yield: About 6 dozen

For an elegant dessert, make a roll by arranging these baked cookies side by side with sweetened whipped cream in between then spread whipped cream over the tops and sides of the roll. Chill 6 to 8 hours before slicing diagonally for striped servings.

• •

1 cup butter or margarine, softened
1/2 cup sugar
1/2 cup brown sugar, packed
2 eggs, slightly beaten
2 3/4 cups flour
1/2 teaspoon baking soda
1 teaspoon salt
2 teaspoons ground cinnamon

Cream butter or margarine with sugar. Add eggs and beat until well blended. Mix in remaining ingredients. Shape into 2 rolls about 2 inches in diameter. Wrap in wax paper and chill several hours or overnight. Cut into 1/8-inch slices. Place slices about 1 inch apart on ungreased baking sheet. Bake. Temperature: 400°F. Time: 6 to 8 minutes or until light brown. Cool. Store in airtight container.

Slice & Bake Cookies

Chocolate Refrigerator Cookies

Yield: About 2-1/2 dozen

*Bake a batch of these and take a handful to bed for your bedtime snack…
'onolicious with scoops of ice cream. These crispy cookies can be the basis of
an endless number of desserts.*

1 cup butter or margarine, softened
$1/2$ cup sugar
$1/2$ cup brown sugar, packed
2 eggs, slightly beaten
$1 1/2$ teaspoons vanilla extract
$2 3/4$ cups flour
$1/2$ teaspoon baking soda
1 teaspoon salt
Colored sugars and decorettes

Mix butter or margarine and sugars together thoroughly in medium mixer bowl. Add egg and vanilla; mix well. Sift together flour, baking soda, and salt; stir into butter mixture and mix until well blended. Mold into a long smooth roll about 2-1/2 inches in diameter. Wrap in wax paper, and chill until firm for several hours or overnight. Using a sharp knife, cut in 1/8-inch thick slices. Place slices about 2 inches apart on ungreased baking sheet. Sprinkle with decorettes or colored sugars, if desired. Bake. Temperature: 400°F. Time: 6 to 8 minutes. Cool. Store in airtight container.

Chocolate Pinwheels

Yield: About 5 dozen

Another old-time favorite that offers an unusual, tasty delight. The contrast of dark and light is an interesting addition to any cookie platter and cookie jar.

. . . .

1/4 cup butter, softened
1/4 cup shortening
3/4 cup sugar
1 egg
1 tablespoon milk
3/4 teaspoon vanilla extract
1 1/4 cups flour
1/4 teaspoon baking powder
1/4 teaspoon salt
1 (1-ounce) square unsweetened chocolate, melted and cooled

Mix together butter, shortening, sugar, and egg until creamy. Stir in milk and vanilla. Mix together and stir in flour, baking powder, and salt to butter mixture; mix until just blended. Divide dough into 2 equal parts. Into one part, blend in melted chocolate. Chill. Roll out white dough into a 9 × 12-inch rectangle on floured surface. Roll out chocolate dough to same size and lay on top of white dough. Roll the double layer of dough gently until 3/16 inch thick. Roll up tightly, beginning at wide side, into logs 12 inches long and 2 inches in diameter; wrap in wax paper and chill several hours or overnight. Slice 1/8 inch thick with sharp knife. Place slices 1 inch apart on lightly greased baking sheet. Bake. Temperature: 350°F. Time: 10 to 12 minutes.

Slice & Bake Cookies

Left: Chocolate Pinwheels
Right: Chocolate Crinkles (see page 78)
Bottom Right: Cornflake Cookies (see page 79)

Macadamia Nut Krispies

Yield: About 6 dozen

The macadamia nuts impart a delicious nutty flavor to these cookies. They make a delightful late night snack with a mug of hot coffee or chocolate.

• •

1 cup butter or margarine, softened
$2/_3$ cup powdered sugar
1 teaspoon vanilla extract
$2^1/_4$ cups flour
$1/_4$ teaspoon salt
$1^1/_4$ cups macadamia nut bits

In a large mixer bowl, cream butter or margarine and sugar. Stir in vanilla. Mix in flour, salt, and nuts. Shape dough into 2 rolls, about 2 inches in diameter; wrap in wax paper and chill for several hours or overnight. Cut into 1/4-inch thick slices; place slices 2 inches apart on baking sheet lined with parchment paper. Bake. Temperature: 350°F. Time: 12 to 15 minutes or light golden brown. Cool. Store in airtight container.

Orange Nut Crisps

Yield: About 8 dozen

There is nothing more comforting and delicious than warm, freshly baked cookies. This is a crisp refrigerator cookie dough that will keep frozen for 2 to 3 months…handy to have ready when the mood to bake hits.

• •

1 cup butter or margarine, softened
1/2 cup brown sugar, packed
1/2 cup sugar
1 egg, beaten
2 tablespoons orange zest
2 tablespoons fresh orange juice
2 3/4 cups flour
1/4 teaspoon baking soda
1/4 teaspoon salt
1/2 cup chopped nuts

Cream together butter or margarine and sugars. Add egg, orange zest, and juice. Add dry ingredients, sifted together, and nuts; mix until blended. Shape dough into 2 long rolls, 2 inches in diameter. Wrap each roll in wax paper and chill several hours or overnight. Cut rolls into 1/8-inch slices with a sharp knife. Place 1 inch apart on ungreased baking sheet. Bake. Temperature: 400°F. Time: 7 minutes or until light brown. Cool. Store in airtight container.

Tip:
For fancy shapes, divide dough into 4 or 6 portions. Place each portion between 2 sheets of wax paper. Roll dough to 1/8-inch thickness. Chill. Cut into various shapes with cookie cutter. Bake as directed above.

Slice & Bake Cookies **103**

Cocoa-Mints

Yield: About 7 dozen

. . . .

3/4 cup butter or margarine, softened
1 cup sugar
1 egg, beaten
2 cups flour
1 teaspoon baking powder
$1/2$ teaspoon baking soda
$1/2$ teaspoon salt
$3/4$ cup cocoa
$1/4$ cup milk
$1/2$ teaspoon vanilla extract

Mint Filling:
3 tablespoons butter, softened
$1^{1}/_{2}$ cups powdered sugar
3 tablespoons milk
4 drops mint flavoring
Green food coloring

Cream together butter or margarine and sugar until light and fluffy. Add egg and beat well. Sift together flour, baking powder, baking soda, salt, and cocoa; add to creamed mixture with milk and vanilla. Shape dough into 2 long rolls, 2 inches in diameter. Wrap each roll in wax paper and chill several hours or overnight. Cut rolls into 1/8-inch slices with a sharp knife. Place 1 inch apart on ungreased baking sheet. Bake. Temperature: 325°F. Time: 10 minutes or until light brown. Remove from baking sheet while still warm. When cooled, put cookies together, sandwich style with Mint Filling.

To prepare Mint Filling, combine all ingredients and beat until smooth and creamy. Spread on one side of a cookie; top with a second cookie. Repeat until all cookies in the batch have been assembled. Store in air-tight container with wax paper between layers of cookies.

Brown Sugar-Nutty Rounds

Yield: About 5 dozen

These are one of the best-loved cookies. The log of dough can be rolled in chopped nuts before chilling or dip half of a baked and cooled cookie in melted chocolate and sprinkle with chopped nuts. Sooooo delicious!

1 cup shortening, softened
$1/2$ cup butter, softened
$1 1/4$ cups brown sugar, packed
$1/2$ teaspoon baking soda
$1/4$ teaspoon salt
1 egg, slightly beaten
1 teaspoon vanilla extract
$2 1/2$ cups flour
$1/2$ cup toasted ground nuts (pecans, hazelnuts, macadamia)

Beat shortening and butter in large mixer bowl for 30 seconds. Add brown sugar, baking soda, and salt; beat until combined. Beat in egg and vanilla until combined. Stir in flour and ground nuts. Divide dough and shape into two 10-inch rolls, 2 inches in diameter on lightly floured surface. Wrap each roll in wax paper or plastic wrap. Chill for 4 to 48 hours or until firm enough to slice. Cut dough into 1/4-inch thick slices using a thin-bladed sharp knife. Place slices 1 inch apart on ungreased baking sheets. Bake. Temperature: 375°F. Time: 8 to 10 minutes or until edges are light brown and firm. Cool completely. Store in airtight containers.

ROLLED & CUT-OUT COOKIES

These cookies get their well-defined shapes from special tools like cookie cutters, a sharp knife, or a pastry wheel to obtain their pretty, fluted edge. Cut-out cookies are made by rolling out the dough with a rolling pin, then cutting it into plain or fancy shapes with the various cookie cutters. Once the cookies are cut, they may be filled in a number of ways to produce an array of fancy creations.

These savory cookies may be frosted, piped, and decorated with colored sugar, miniature candies, and other kinds of decorettes. Occasionally, they are used like an artist's "canvas" and designs are hand-painted.

Tips for Rolled
& Cut-out Cookies

- Lightly roll a small amount of dough at a time, keeping the rest chilled.
- Roll dough very thin for crisp cookies.
- Cut as many cookies from each rolling as possible.
- Dip cookie cutter in flour, shake it, and cut.
- Most of the cut-out cookies may be frosted or decorated.
- Instead of rolling the dough, drop dough onto baking sheet and flatten with a glass dipped in flour—a short cut when in a hurry.
- Use wide spatula to lift dough onto baking sheet.
- To help prevent dough from sticking, sprinkle rolling surface with flour and rub flour onto rolling pin. Too much flour and rerolling the dough results in dry, tough cookies.

Cut-Out Butter Cookies

Yield: About 6 dozen

This simple butter cookie recipe is perfect for making cut-out cookies with children. This traditional recipe is simple and the decorating possibilities are endless. Try it, you'll love it!

1 cup sugar
1 cup butter, softened
1/4 cup milk
1 egg, slightly beaten
1 teaspoon vanilla extract
3 cups flour
1/2 teaspoon baking powder
1/4 teaspoon baking soda

Combine sugar and butter in large mixer bowl and beat at medium speed until light and fluffy, about 1 to 2 minutes. Add milk, egg, and vanilla; continue beating until well mixed. Add flour, baking powder, and baking soda and beat additional 2 to 3 minutes on low. Cover; refrigerate 1 hour or until firm. Roll out half the dough on lightly floured surface to 1/8-inch thickness. Cut out with 2-inch cutters and place 1 inch apart on ungreased baking sheets. Repeat with the remaining refrigerated dough. Bake. Temperature: 375°F. Time: 5 to 7 minutes or until edges are light brown. Cool completely. Frost and decorate (see Decorating page) cooled cookies as desired.

Sugar Cookies

Yield: About 5 dozen

Children love these cookies and the many fancy shapes
they can make while helping to bake them.

3/4 cup butter or margarine, softened
1 cup sugar
2 eggs
1 teaspoon vanilla extract
2 3/4 cups flour
1 teaspoon baking powder
1 teaspoon salt
Sugar for sprinkling
Decorettes, optional

In large mixer bowl beat butter or margarine and 1 cup sugar until light and fluffy; beat in eggs and vanilla until well blended. In another bowl, stir together flour, baking powder, and salt; gradually add to butter mixture, blending well, to form a soft dough. Cover with plastic wrap and refrigerate until firm, about 1 to 2 hours or up to 3 days. Roll dough out on floured board, a portion at a time, to 1/8-inch thickness (keep remaining portions refrigerated). Cut into desired shapes with cookie cutter(s) and place slightly apart on ungreased baking sheets. Sprinkle generously with sugar or decorettes. Bake. Temperature: 400°F. Time: 8 to 10 minutes or until edges are lightly browned. Cool. Store in airtight container. These cookies are frequently frosted and/or decorated for special occasions (see Decorating page).

Variation:

Lemon Sugar Cookies: Use 2 teaspoons lemon zest plus 1 teaspoon fresh lemon juice instead of vanilla. Bake as directed above.

Lime Zingers
Yield: About 72

These tangy cookies became an instant hit when they were prize winners!

. . . .

1 cup butter, softened
$1/2$ cup sugar
2 teaspoons lime zest
$1/4$ cup lime juice
1 teaspoon vanilla
$2 1/4$ cups flour
$3/4$ cup finely chopped nuts (macadamia, hazelnut, Brazil)

Frosting:
$1/2$ of an 8-ounce package cream cheese, softened
1 cup sifted powdered sugar
1 tablespoon lime juice
1 teaspoon vanilla extract
Food coloring

To prepare cookies, beat butter and sugar in large mixer bowl until combined. Beat in lime zest, lime juice, and vanilla. Stir in flour and nuts; mix until thoroughly blended. Divide dough in half. Roll half of the dough on lightly floured surface to about 1/4-inch thickness. Using 1- or 2-inch cookie cutters, cut into desired shapes. Place on ungreased cookie sheets. Bake. Temperature: 350°F. Time: 8 to 10 minutes or until edges are light brown. Cool on wire rack.

For frosting, combine all Frosting ingredients; mix on medium speed until smooth. Tint frosting as desired with food coloring. Frost cooled cookies just before serving.

Brown Sugar Shortbreads

Yield: About 3 dozen

These cookies acquire an appealing crunch as they cool. It only takes four ingredients to make them—simple!

1 cup butter or margarine, softened
1$\frac{1}{4}$ cups brown sugar, packed
$\frac{3}{4}$ teaspoon vanilla extract
2$\frac{1}{2}$ cups flour
Sugar for sprinkling, optional

Beat butter or margarine and sugar until light and fluffy in large mixer bowl. Add vanilla; then gradually beat in flour, blending thoroughly. Gather dough into a ball; wrap in plastic wrap and refrigerate until firm, about 1 to 2 hours or up to 3 days. Roll out dough on lightly floured board to 1/4-inch thickness. Cut out desired shapes with cookie cutters dipped in flour and place about 1 inch apart on lightly greased baking sheets. If desired, sprinkle with sugar or decorate after cooled. Bake. Temperature: 300°F. Time: 35 to 40 minutes or until firm to the touch (press very lightly to test). Transfer to racks and let cool. Store in airtight container.

Stained Glass Cookies

*When the hard candy melts in the "window" of these cookies,
it looks like "stained glass" on their buttery surface.*

3/4 cup sugar
1 cup butter, softened
1 (3-ounce) package cream cheese, softened
1 egg, slightly beaten
1 teaspoon vanilla extract
3 cups flour

Decorations:

Fruit-flavored hard candies, unwrapped and crushed
Decorator sugars and candies

Combine sugar, butter, cream cheese, egg, and vanilla in large mixer bowl. Beat at medium speed, scraping bowl often, 2 to 3 minutes or until creamy. Reduce mixer speed to low; add flour and beat just until mixed, 1 to 2 minutes. Divide dough in half; cover and refrigerate several hours or overnight.

On lightly floured surface, roll out half the dough, keeping remaining dough refrigerated, into a 15 × 10-inch rectangle. Cut dough into about twenty 3 × 2-1/2-inch rectangles using a sharp knife or pastry wheel. Cut small shapes in the center of each rectangle using tiny cookie cutters or a sharp knife. Save cut-out shapes to decorate remaining dough; place on aluminum foil-lined baking sheets. (If using more than one color candy, keep candy separated by color. When filling holes, mix colors as little as possible). Bake. Temperature: 325°F. Time: 7 to 9 minutes or until edges are very light brown and candy is melted. Cool completely before removing from baking sheets.

Pistachio Butter Cookies

Yield: About 6 dozen

*If you like pistachio nuts, you'll love these cookies. They're the
perfect match to a good cup of coffee or tea.*

1 cup sugar
1 cup butter, softened
2 eggs, slightly beaten
2 teaspoons vanilla extract
2³/₄ cups flour
1¹/₄ cups finely chopped salted pistachios, toasted
¹/₄ teaspoon salt
1 egg white
1 tablespoon water

Beat together sugar and butter in large mixer bowl at medium speed 1
to 2 minutes or until light and fluffy. Add 2 eggs and vanilla; continue
beating until well mixed. Reduce speed to low and add flour, 1 cup pistachios, and salt; beat until well mixed. Divide dough in half; wrap in
plastic food wrap and refrigerate 1 to 2 hours or until firm.

Roll out dough, half at a time, on lightly floured surface to 1/4-inch
thickness. Cut with 2-1/2-inch round cutter; cut each round in half and
place 1 inch apart on greased baking sheets. In small bowl, beat together egg white and water; brush tops of cookies lightly with egg mixture
and sprinkle with remaining pistachios. Bake. Temperature: 350°F. Time:
10 to 12 minutes or until edges are light brown. Cool. Store in airtight
container.

Frostings

Fancy frostings can make your cookies miniature works of art. It is also a wonderful activity for children to express their creativity.

Frosting and Decorating Tips:
- Cool cookies completely before frosting.
- Use disposable decorating bags for easy clean-up.
- Have a few basic decorating tips handy—a small writing tip, a star tip, and a small rose tip for special touches.
- The frosting consistency should be thick enough to hold the piping shape but thin enough to squeeze easily from the bag.
- Use frosting made with shortening instead of butter for brightest colors.
- Liquid or paste food coloring may be used; paste gives a more intense color without thinning the frosting.
- Squeeze frosting from the end of the decorating bag and use steady pressure to keep the frosting flowing evenly.
- Let frosted cookies stand on rack until frosting is firm.
- Store in single layer in cool, dry place.
- Decorated cookies can be frozen; be sure frosting is dry first to prevent color from bleeding when cookies are thawed.
- To drizzle glazes easily, pour glaze into corner of a heavy food resealable storage bag. Sniff off a tiny corner and squeeze gently while moving it over the food.
- Sprinkle colored sugar, small candies, candied fruit, or nuts over frosted cookies.

Buttercream Frosting

Yield: About 3 cups

A delicious, versatile, creamy, white butter frosting which can easily be adapted to feature numerous flavors.

$3/4$ cup butter, softened
6 cups sifted powdered sugar
$1/8$ teaspoon salt
$1/3$ whipped cream
$3/4$ teaspoon vanilla
2 tablespoons light corn syrup

Beat butter at medium speed in large mixer bowl until creamy, about 1 to 2 minutes. Gradually add powdered sugar and salt alternately with whipping cream and vanilla, scraping bowl frequently, until well blended and of desired consistency. Stir in corn syrup; mix well.

Variations:

Chocolate Frosting: Add 2 to 3 (1-ounce) squares of melted unsweetened baking chocolate.

Lemon or Orange Frosting: Stir in 1 tablespoon lemon or orange zest.

Coconut Frosting: Stir in 1 teaspoon coconut extract or flavoring.

Creamy Butter Frosting

Yield: About 2-1/4 cups

4 cups sifted powdered sugar
$^1/_2$ cup butter, softened
$1^1/_2$ teaspoons vanilla
3 to 4 tablespoons milk
Food coloring, optional

Combine powdered sugar, butter, and vanilla in small mixer bowl. Beat at low speed, gradually adding milk and scraping bowl frequently, until it reaches desired spreading consistency. Color with food coloring, if desired. Decorate cooled cookies or bars. Cover; store refrigerated. Bring to room temperature before using; mix well.

Royal Icing

Yield: About 3/4 cup

This icing hardens when it dries and is used for piping decorations on cooled cookies.

1 1/2 cups sifted powdered sugar
1 tablespoon meringue powder*
2 tablespoons warm water
1/4 teaspoon cream of tartar

Combine all ingredients in large mixer bowl; beat at low speed until moistened. Increase speed to medium; beat until stiff and glossy, about 2 to 3 minutes. If too stiff, add more warm water. Cover icing with damp paper towel or plastic wrap and refrigerate until ready to use; will keep for up to 2 weeks in refrigerator. To restore texture, allow icing to reach room temperature, then rebeat.

*Meringue powder is available in specialty cooking shops and the baking section of large supermarkets.

Powdered Sugar Glaze

Yield: About 1 cup

*This frosting hardens and gives cookies a glazed
surface–perfect for decorating.*

2$\frac{1}{2}$ cups sifted powdered sugar
2 tablespoons water
1 tablespoon light corn syrup
1 tablespoon butter, softened
$\frac{1}{2}$ teaspoon almond or vanilla extract
Food coloring, optional

Combine all ingredients, except food coloring, in small mixer bowl; mix
at low speed until powdered sugar is moistened. Beat at medium speed
until smooth, adding more water if necessary to reach desired spreading consistency. Color with food coloring, if desired. Frost cooled cookies; let stand until hardened (6 hours or overnight).

NO-BAKE COOKIES

When you're expecting guests and the cookie jar is empty, just whip up a recipe of No-Bake Cookies. They're quick and easy to make, most taking only about 20 to 30 minutes to prepare. Since the flavor of some No-Bake Cookies becomes richer over time, these delectable treats can be prepared in advance and will still be delicious days later.

Some No-Bake Cookies are made by combining cookie or cracker crumbs with butter, fruits, or nuts. Toss together and shape into balls and they're ready for the children or adults to enjoy. Use these recipes as a guide to create your own varieties.

These cookies also make great gifts.

Tips for No-Bake Cookies

A range of No-Bake cookies can be made by mixing melted ingredients with dry ingredients and allowing them to set. The agent that sets the cookies may be chocolate, which sets firmly, or syrups and marshmallows, which set to make chewier cookies.

- Combine melted semisweet chocolate, light corn or maple syrup, and butter with breakfast cereals. Crushed or broken plain cookies, dried fruit and nuts may be substituted for cereal.
- Always allow the melted chocolate to cool before adding dry ingredients
- A mixture of cooked sugar or light corn syrup combined with melted butter, marshmallows, and soft toffee may also be used to set No-Bake cookies. The most effective mixture uses equal parts of toffees, butter, and marshmallows mixed with puffed rice cereal.
- No-Bake cookies can be made into rounds (balls), cookie wedges, cookie triangles, or layers.

Rounds: Spoon cookie mixture onto waxed paper to form log; chill until firm and slice or form into walnut-size balls and set onto waxed paper and chill until firm.

Wedges: Spoon cookie mixture into lightly greased and lined shallow round baking pan; chill 1 to 2 hours or until firm. Remove from pan and slice into wedges.

Triangles: Spoon cookie mixture into plastic wrap-lined 7-inch square pan; let stand until firm then chill until set. Remove mixture from pan, peel off plastic wrap and cut into triangular slices.

Layered: Most No-Bake cookies are single layered. If making more than one layer, remember that you need to be able to slice through the cookies cleanly to avoid crumbling.

Fudge Balls

Yield: About 3 dozen

*The flavor of these treats becomes richer after a few days
so make these a day or two in advance.*

2 cups crushed chocolate graham crackers
1 cup powdered sugar
$1/_2$ cup finely chopped nuts
$1/_4$ cup butter, melted
1 tablespoon almond extract
3 tablespoons water
Multicolored sugar or powdered sugar

In a large bowl combine graham crackers, 1 cup powdered sugar, nuts, butter, almond extract, and water; mix well. Shape mixture into 1-inch balls; roll in colored sugar or additional powdered sugar. Place on wax paper, cover, and refrigerate at least 1 hour. Roll again in additional multicolored sugar just before serving. Store any leftovers in a covered container in refrigerator.

Frosted Ginger Cookies

Yield: 24 cookies

Give a special touch to store-bought cookies with this lemony frosting.

2 cups powdered sugar
2 tablespoons butter, softened
1$\frac{1}{2}$ teaspoons lemon zest
2 to 3 tablespoons milk

48 thin ginger cookies, purchased

In a small bowl combine powdered sugar, butter, and lemon zest. Gradually add milk while beating at low speed until of desired frosting consistency. Spread about 1 to 2 teaspoons frosting onto flat side of 1 cookie; top with second cookie, flat-side down. Press together gently to make a sandwich cookie.

Variations:

Frosted Vanilla or Chocolate Cookies: substitute vanilla or chocolate wafers for ginger cookies.

No-Bake Chocolate Drop Cookies

Yield: About 2 dozen

These no-bake cookies are a snap to make!

1$\frac{1}{2}$ cups quick-cooking oatmeal
$\frac{1}{2}$ cup flaked coconut
$\frac{1}{4}$ cup chopped nuts
$\frac{3}{4}$ cup sugar
$\frac{1}{4}$ cup butter
$\frac{1}{4}$ cup milk
$\frac{1}{4}$ cup unsweetened cocoa

Flaked coconut, if desired

In medium bowl, combine oatmeal, coconut, and nuts; set aside. In 2-quart saucepan, combine sugar, butter, milk, and cocoa. Cook over medium heat, stirring occasionally, until mixture comes to a full boil, about 3 to 4 minutes. Cook 1 minute; remove from heat and stir in oats mixture. Drop mixture by rounded teaspoonfuls onto wax paper-lined cookie sheet. Roll in additional coconut while warm. Cool completely and store refrigerated.

Cherry Date Coconut Drops

Yield: About 4-1/2 dozen

A rich combination of fruits and nuts are dropped in coconut to make a wholesome treat.

$^2/_3$ cup butter
1 cup brown sugar, packed
1 (8-ounce) package dates, chopped
1 egg
1 tablespoon vanilla
3 cups crisp rice cereal
$^1/_2$ cup chopped macadamia nuts
$^1/_4$ cup chopped maraschino cherries, drained
$2^1/_2$ cups flaked coconut

Melt butter in skillet; stir in brown sugar and dates; remove from heat. Add egg and cook over medium heat, stirring constantly, until mixture comes to a full boil, about 4 to 6 minutes. Cook 1 more minute, stirring constantly; remove from heat. Add all remaining ingredients except coconut; stir until moistened and let stand 5 minutes. Place coconut in medium bowl. Shape rounded teaspoonfuls of date mixture into balls; roll in coconut. Place on wax paper-lined cookie sheets and allow to set, about 30 to 60 minutes. Store in refrigerator.

Chocolate Dreams

Yield: About 8 dozen

Easy to make cookies that are rich and chewy. These cookies are best eaten on the same day they are made.

$^1/_2$ cup butter or margarine
2 (1-ounce) squares unsweetened chocolate
2 cups sugar
$^1/_2$ cup milk
1 teaspoon vanilla
1 cup chopped nuts
1 cup fresh or frozen shredded coconut
3 cups quick-cooking oatmeal

Melt butter and chocolate in saucepan. Add sugar and milk; cook over medium heat 5 minutes, stirring constantly. Remove from heat and blend in vanilla, nuts, and coconut; fold in oatmeal. Drop by teaspoonfuls onto wax paper; refrigerate until firm, about 1 hour. Serve as soon as possible.

Peanut Butter Bars

Yield: About 18 bars

Crispy cookie bars that are easy to make and delicious.
It is the perfect recipe for young bakers.

1/4 cup butter or margarine
1/2 cup peanut butter
1/2 pound marshmallows
5 cups dry cereal of choice

Combine butter or margarine, peanut butter, and marshmallows; melt over hot water or microwave 10 to 15 seconds until melted. Place cereal in large bowl; stir in peanut butter mixture. Toss to blend well. Spoon evenly into 9 × 9-inch pan greased with butter or margarine. Press down slightly; cool in pan. Cut into bars to serve. Store in airtight container placing wax paper between layers to prevent sticking.

Cocoa Oatmeal Cookies

Yield: About 36

This has been my recipe for more than 25 years, and I enjoyed making them even as a child. My grandchildren enjoy making them, too.

2 cups sugar
$1/_3$ cup unsweetened cocoa
$1/_2$ cup butter or margarine
$1/_2$ cup milk
1 teaspoon vanilla extract
3 cups uncooked quick-cooking oatmeal (not instant)
Hot water, if needed

Combine sugar, cocoa, butter or margarine, and milk in a 3-quart saucepan. Cook, stirring constantly, over medium heat until mixture comes to a boil; continue cooking for 6 to 7 minutes, stirring constantly. Remove from heat; stir in vanilla and oatmeal. Drop by tablespoonfuls onto wax paper. If mixture begins to get sugary before finishing, add a few drops of hot water and stir until mixture is of proper consistency. Continue until all the mixture has been used. Best eaten soon after they are made.

Chocolate Macadamia Clusters

Yield: About 3 dozen

These candy-like cookies are easy to make, especially for
children who will enjoy these sweet treats.

1 (12-ounce) package semi-sweet chocolate pieces
1 tablespoon vegetable shortening
3 cups wheat cereal flakes (bran flakes, cornflakes)
1 cup macadamia nut bits
$1/_2$ cup sweetened flaked coconut

Melt chocolate pieces and shortening in 3-quart saucepan over low heat, stirring occasionally, until smooth, about 5 to 8 minutes. Stir in remaining ingredients until well coated. Drop by rounded teaspoonfuls onto wax paper. Cover; refrigerate 1 hour or until set. Store covered and refrigerated.

Hawaiian Energy Bars

Yield: About 36 bars

Nothing like having a batch of wholesome cookies for children to snack on when the munchies hit.

$2^1/_2$ cups crisp rice cereal
$1^1/_2$ cups quick-cooking oatmeal
$^1/_4$ cup toasted sesame seeds
1 (10-ounce) package marshmallows
$^1/_2$ cup creamy peanut butter
$^1/_4$ cup butter or margarine
$^3/_4$ cup chopped macadamia nuts
1 cup raisins
$^3/_4$ cup shredded coconut

In a 2-quart saucepan, combine rice cereal, oatmeal, and sesame seeds; toast over medium heat a few minutes; set aside. In a large saucepan, combine marshmallows, peanut butter, and butter or margarine; melt over low heat stirring constantly. Stir in cereal mixture, macadamia nuts, raisins, and coconut. Press firmly into greased 13 × 9 × 2-inch pan. Let stand and cool completely; cut into bars.

Rum Balls

Yield: About 4 dozen

These cookies are great to have on hand anytime you're entertaining!

8 vanilla wafers
1 cup finely chopped dried fruit(s) (raisins, apricots, prunes, dates, figs)
1 (14-ounce) can sweetened condensed milk
3 cups unsweetened shredded coconut
Zest of 1 lemon
2 tablespoons lemon juice
1 tablespoon unsweetened cocoa powder
1 tablespoon dark rum

Finely crush wafers in food processor. In a large bowl, combine wafers, dried fruit(s), condensed milk, 1 cup of coconut, lemon peel and juice, cocoa, and rum. With wet hands shape mixture into 1-inch balls and roll in remaining 2 cups of shredded coconut. Store in airtight containers in the refrigerator.

PART 3

APPENDICES

Glossary of Cooking Terms

Bake: Cook in oven surrounded by dry heat.

Batter: An uncooked mixture of flour, eggs, and liquid with other ingredients; thin enough to be spooned or poured.

Blanch: Plunge food into boiling water for a brief time to preserve color, texture, and nutritional value or to remove skin from fruits, nuts, or vegetables.

Blend: Combine ingredients with spoon, wire whisk, or rubber scraper until very smooth and uniform.

Boil: Heat liquid until bubbles rise continuously and break on surface. Rolling boil, bubbles form rapidly.

Caramelize: Melt sugar slowly over low heat until it becomes a golden-brown, caramel flavored syrup. Or, sprinkle sugar on top of food and apply heat until sugar is melted and caramelized.

Chop: Cut into coarse or fine irregular pieces.

Coat: Cover food evenly with crumbs or sauce.

Cool: Allow hot food to stand at room temperature for specified amount of time.

Core: Remove the center of a fruit.

Crush: Press into very fine particles.

Cube: Cut food into squares ½ inch or larger.

Cut-in: Distribute solid fat in dry ingredients until particles are desired size using fork, two knives, or pastry blender.

Cut-up: Cut into irregular or smaller pieces.

Dash: Less than ⅛ teaspoon of an ingredient.

Dice: Cut food into squares smaller than ½ inch.

Dissolve: Stir a dry ingredient into a liquid ingredient until dry ingredient melts or disappears.

Dot: Drop small pieces of an ingredient randomly over food.

Dough: Mixture of flour and liquid with other ingredients; it is stiff but pliable.

Drain: Pour off liquid by placing food into a strainer or colander.

Drizzle: Pour topping in thin lines from a spoon or liquid measure in an uneven pattern over food.

Dust: Sprinkle lightly with flour, cornmeal, powdered sugar, or cocoa.

Flake: Break lightly into small pieces, using fork.

Flute: Squeeze pastry edge with fingers to make an ornamental design.

Fold: Combine ingredients lightly while preventing loss of air by using two motions—first cut down vertically through mixture with spatula then slide spatula across bottom of bowl and up the side, turning mixture over.

Glaze: Brush, spread, or drizzle an ingredient or mixture of ingredients on hot or cold foods to give a glossy appearance.

Grate: Rub food again the holes of a grater to produce tiny particles.

Grease: Rubbing the surface of a pan with shortening; using pastry brush, waxed paper, or paper towel to prevent food from sticking during baking.

Grease and Flour: Rubbing the inside surface of a pan with shortening before dusting with flour.

Heat Oven: Turn on oven controls to desired temperature, allowing oven to heat before baking. Preheating.

Knead: Work dough on floured surface into a smooth, elastic mass.

Mince: Cut food into very fine pieces; smaller than chopped food.

Mix: Combine ingredients in any way that distributes them evenly.

Peel: Remove outer covering of fruits or vegetables.

Process: Use either food processor or mini chopper to liquefy, blend, chop, grind, or knead food.

Reduce: Boil liquid uncovered to evaporate liquid and intensify flavor.

Shred: Cut into long, thin pieces.

Slice: Cut into uniform-size flat pieces.

Stir: Combine ingredients with circular or figure-eight motion until uniform consistency.

Soft Peaks: Egg whites beaten until peaks are rounded or curl when beaters are lifted from bowl while still moist and glossy.

Soften: Let cold food stand at room temperature, or microwave at low power setting, until no longer hard.

Stiff Peaks: Egg whites beaten until peaks stand up straight when beaters are lifted from bowl.

Strain: Pour mixture or liquid through a fine sieve or strainer to remove larger particles.

Tear: Break into pieces by hand.

Toss: Tumble ingredients lightly with lifting motion.

Whip: Beat ingredients to add air and increase volume until light and fluffy.

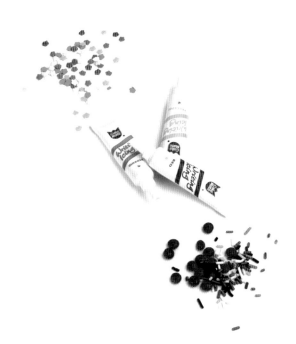

Primary Cookie Ingredients

Most cookies are made from butter, sugar, flour, and sometimes eggs and other ingredients and flavorings. To make the best cookies, always use fresh, quality ingredients.

BUTTER & FATS

Butter: Sweet butter (salted or unsalted) is best for making cookies.

Lard: Opaque white fat made from rendered pork fat and used in traditional British recipes.

Margarine: Usually less expensive than butter and can be used in the same way but won't produce the same flavor as butter.

Vegetable Oil: May sometimes be used instead of solid fat. It is an economical blend of oils from various vegetables, such as corn, safflower, cottonseed, peanut, and soybean. They are used in both cooking and baking.

Shortening: Made from blended vegetable oils, usually soybean and cottonseed. It is flavorless and creates light, short-textured cookies.

SUGAR & OTHER SWEETNERS

Corn Syrup: Slightly less sweet than sugar; often used in no-bake recipes.

Honey: Best to use blended honey in cookie dough; flavor of milder honeys will be lost.

Malt Syrup: Dark, concentrated syrup made from corn and barley with a distinctive flavor and thick consistency.

Maple Syrup: A syrup from the maple tree, thinner than golden syrup, with a distinctive flavor.

Molasses: A by-product of sugar refining; has a slightly bitter flavor.

Sugar: Many different types of sweetener are available, each adding its distinctive character to cookies.

- Refined sugar: Made from sugarcane and sugar beet; refined white sugar is 99.9% pure sucrose.
- Granulated sugar: Has large granules; used most often cookie recipes.
- Superfine sugar: Ideal for creaming with butter
- Confectioners' sugar: Fine, powdery sugar used to make icings and fillings; also used to dust cookies; also known as powdered sugar.
- Brown sugar: Refined white sugar tossed in molasses or syrup to color and flavor; the darker the color, the more intense the flavor, making moister cookies. Never substitute white or brown sugar for the other.
- Raw sugar: Rich golden sugar with a slight toffee flavor; large grains; used in cookie dough if crunchy texture is required. Good for sprinkling over cookies before baking.

WHEAT FLOURS

All-Purpose Flour: Most cookie recipes use all-purpose flour as it has a low gluten content resulting in a crumbly texture.

Bread Flour: Wheat high in gluten-forming protein than all-purpose flour, which gives more structure to bread. It is best used for yeast breads and bread machine breads. For other kinds of baking, bread flour can make some recipes too tough.

Cake Flour: Milled from soft wheat and lower in protein than all-purpose flour, cake flour results in tender, fine-textured cakes. Not recommended as a substitute for either all-purpose or bread flour.

Rye Flour: Milled from rye grain and low in gluten-forming protein. It is usually combined with wheat flour to increase the dough's gluten-forming capabilities.

Self-Rising Flour: This flour contains raising agents that make cookies spread and rise, giving them a lighter texture. For every one cup of all-purpose flour, add one teaspoon baking powder to substitute for one cup self-rising flour.

Whole-Wheat Flour: Milled from the entire wheat kernel and contains all the nutrients and flavor of wheat; coarser than white flour, gives heavier result and absorbs more liquid than white flour.

NON-WHEAT FLOURS

These flours can be great for cookies, too, although some should be combined with wheat flour.

Chestnut Flour: Made from ground chestnuts; light brown with a nutty flavor.

Cornmeal: Also known as polenta or maize meal; bright yellow with a coarse or medium-ground texture.

Cornstarch: Made from the middle of the maize kernel; fine white powder.

Potato Flour: Made from potato starch and may be mixed with wheat flour to create lighter texture to cookies.

Rice Flour: Made by finely grinding polished white rice; used in many cookie recipes to give a short, slightly crumbly texture.

Soy Flour: Made from soybeans; has distinctive nutty flavor; medium to low-fat varieties available.

LEAVENING AGENTS

Leavening or raising agents react upon contact with water and produce carbon dioxide bubbles that make the cookies rise during baking. Therefore, cookie dough containing leavening agents must be shaped and baked as soon as liquid is added.

Baking Powder: Mixture of alkaline baking soda and an acid such as cream of tartar.

Baking Soda: This can be added to a cookie mixture that contains an acidic ingredient.

MILK

Usually refers to cow's milk in most cookbooks.

Buttermilk: Thick, smooth liquid that results when skim or part-skim milk is cultured with lactic acid bacteria. Used in baking for a tangy flavor.

Evaporated Milk: Whole milk with more than half of the water removed before mixture is homogenized. Mixture is slightly thicker than whole milk. Use "as is" in recipes called for evaporated milk or mix with equal volume of water to substitute for whole milk.

Low-fat Milk: Contains 0.5 to 2% butterfat.

Skim Milk: Contains less than 0.5% butterfat.

Sweetened Condensed Milk: Made when about half of the water is removed from whole milk and sweetener is added.

Whole Milk: Contains at least 3.25% butterfat.

EGGS

Eggs are used to enrich cookie dough and bind dry ingredients. For baking, eggs should be at room temperature; cold egg yolks may curdle and cold egg whites will produce less volume when whisked. Add eggs to creamed mixture one at a time, beating after each addition and add 1 tablespoon sifted flour to the mixture if it starts to curdle. Always whisk egg whites in a clean bowl and use immediately.

FRUITS, NUTS, AND SEEDS

Dried and candied fruits, nuts, and seeds may be added to cookie dough to add flavor, texture, and color. Sprinkle them over unbaked cookies. Always purchase really fresh nuts in small quantities and chop as needed. Store them in airtight containers in the refrigerator or freezer.

Weights & Measures

EQUVALENT MEASUREMENTS

1/8 cup (1 fluid ounce)	=	2 tablespoons
1/4 cup (2 fluid ounces)	=	4 tablespoons
1/3 cup	=	5-1/3 tablespoons
1/2 cup (4 fluid ounces)	=	8 tablespoons
3/4 cup (6 fluid ounces)	=	12 tablespoons
1 cup (8 fluid ounces)	=	16 tablespoons or 1/2 pint
2 cups (16 fluid ounces)	=	1 pint
1 quart (32 fluid ounces)	=	2 pints
1/2 gallon (64 fluid ounces)	=	2 quarts
1 gallon (128 fluid ounces)	=	4 quarts

HELPFUL FOOD EQUIVALENTS

1/2 cup butter	=	1 stick butter
1 square baking chocolate	=	1 ounce chocolate
6 ounces chocolate chips	=	1 cup chocolate chips
2-1/4 cups packed brown sugar	=	1 pound brown sugar
3-1/2 cups confectioners sugar	=	1 pound confectioners sugar
2 cups granulated sugar	=	1 pound granulated sugar
4 cups all-purpose flour	=	1 pound all-purpose flour

Quick Substitutions

*Use these substitutions only in a pinch as they may affect
the flavor or texture of your recipe.*

INSTEAD OF THIS...	USE THIS...
Apple pie spice, 1 teaspoon	1/2 tsp. ground cinnamon plus 1/4 tsp. ground nutmeg, 1/8 tsp. ground allspice and dash ground cloves or ginger.
Baking powder, 1 teaspoon	1/4 tsp. baking soda plus 1/2 tsp. cream of tartar
Butter, 1 cup	1 cup margarine or 1 cup hydrogenated fat plus 1/2 tsp. salt
Buttermilk or sour milk, 1 cup	1 tbsp. vinegar or lemon juice plus sweet milk to make 1 cup (let stand 5 minutes before using) or 1 cup plain yogurt.
Cake flour, 1 cup	1 cup minus 2 tbsp. all-purpose flour
Chocolate, semisweet 1 ounce	3 tbsp. semisweet chocolate pieces or 1 oz. unsweetened chocolate plus 1 tbsp. sugar.
Chocolate, sweet baking, 4 ounces	1/4 cup unsweetened cocoa powder plus 1/3 cup sugar and 3 tbsp. shortening.
Chocolate, unsweetened, 1 ounce	3 tbsp. unsweetened cocoa powder plus 1 tbsp. cooking oil or shortening, melted.
Cream, light 1 cup	1 tbsp. melted butter plus enough whole milk to make 1 cup.

Quick Substitutions

INSTEAD OF THIS...	USE THIS...
Cream, whipped 1 cup	2 cups whipped dessert topping or 1 cup evaporated milk, chilled until ice crystals form plus 1 tsp. lemon juice
Egg, whole 1	2 egg yolks or 2 egg whites or 1/4 cup egg substitute
Flour (as thickener), 1 tablespoon	1/2 tbsp. cornstarch, potato starch, or rice starch
Flour, cake 1 cup	1 cup minus 2 tbsp. all-purpose flour
Flour, self-rising 1 cup	1 cup all-purpose flour plus 1 tsp. baking powder, 1/2 tsp. salt and 1/4 tsp. baking soda.
Ginger root, grated 1 teaspoon	1/4 tsp. ground ginger
Honey, 1 cup	1-1/4 cups sugar plus 1/4 cup water
Mascarpone cheese, 8 ounces	8 ounces regular cream cheese
Milk, whole 1 cup	1/2 cup evaporated milk plus 1/2 cup water or 1 cup water plus 1/3 cup nonfat dry milk powder
Molasses, 1 cup	1 cup honey
Pumpkin pie spice, 1 teaspoon	1/2 tsp. ground cinnamon plus 1/4 tsp. ground ginger, 1/4 tsp. ground allspice and 1/8 tsp. ground nutmeg.
Sour cream, dairy 1 cup	1 cup plain yogurt
Sugar, granulated 1 cup	1 cup packed brown sugar or 2 cups sifted powdered sugar

Index of Recipes

Bars & Brownies

Apricot-Coconut Bars	16
Apricot Bars	25
Banana Bars with Orange Butter Icing	17
Blondies	33
Buttery Hawaiian Lemon Bars	27
Chocolate Chip Blondies	33
Chocolate Chip Brownies	37
Chocolate Coconut Bars	28
Chocolate Kisses Brownies	37
Cream Cheese Brownies	38
Date Bars	25
Date Oatmeal Bars	32
Favorite Brownies	37
Fig Bars	25
Fruit Bars	24
Guava Bars	30
Hawaiian Fruit Bars	19
Macadamia Butter Bars	29
Mac Nut Brownies	37
Mac Nut-Cheesecake Bars	35
Mango Bars	25
Peanut Butter Brownies	36
Pineapple Mac Nut Bars	20
Pineapple Nut Bars	20
Prune Bars	25
Raisin Blondies	33
Toffee Bars	21
Triple Layered Brownies	40
Tsubushian Shortbread	22

Drop Cookies

Alissa's Chocolate Chip Cookies	51
Basic Butter Cookies	47
Chocolate Chips	47
Chocolate Chip Bars	51
Chocolate Macadamia Lace Cookies	63
Chocolate Puffs	56
Coconut Island Cookies	64
Coconut Macaroons	59
Cranberry Cookies	47
Giant Oatmeal Cookies	45
Giant Cranberry Oatmeal Cookies	48
Giant Triple Chocolate Cookies	61
Hawaiian Chocolate Chip	51
Krispy Krunchies	53
Mac Nut Macaroons	57
Macadamia Clusters	60
Macadamia Lace Cookies	63
Nutty Cookies	47
Oatmeal Cinnamon Cookies	48
Oatmeal Raisin Cookies	45
Peanut Butter Cookies	47
Rainbow Cookies	54
Raisin Cookies	47
Stephen's Favorite Oatmeal Cookies	45
Toll Oats Cookies	46
Wholesome Oatmeal Cookies	45

Frostings

Buttercream Frosting	120
Chocolate Frosting	120
Coconut Frosting	120
Lemon Frosting	120

Orange Frosting 120
Creamy Butter Frosting 121
Royal Icing 122
Powdered Sugar Glaze 123

No-Bake Cookies
Cherry Date Coconut Drops 131
Chocolate Dreams 132
Chocolate Macadamia Clusters 135
Cocoa Oatmeal Cookies 134
Frosted Chocolate Cookies 128
Frosted Ginger Cookies 128
Frosted Vanilla Cookies 128
Fudge Balls 126
Hawaiian Energy Bars 136
No-Bake Chocolate Drop
  Cookies 129
Peanut Butter Bars 133
Rum Balls 138

Pressed & Shaped Cookies
Biscotti Toscani 93
Chinese Almond Cookies 80
Chocolate Crinkles 78
Christmas Wreaths 88
Cornflake Cookies 79
Cocoa Kisses 73
Coconut Crisps 83
Cream Cheese Spritz 69
Fortune Cookies 82
Jam Thumbprints 88
Macadamia Nut Cookies 79
Old Fashioned Peanut
  Butter Cookies 85

Oatmeal Crunchies 72
Peanut Blossom Cookies 86
Peanut Butter and Jelly Cookies 85
Potato Chip Cookies 91
Russian Tea Cookies 70
Sesame Seed Cookies 75
Shortbread Cookies 74
Snickerdoodles 90
Soft Ginger Cookies 87
Spritz 68
Tropical Thumbprint Cookies 88
Turtle Cookies 77

Rolled & Cut-Out Cookies
Brown Sugar Shortbreads 113
Cutout Butter Cookies 108
Lemon Sugar Cookies 111
Lime Zingers 112
Pistachio Butter Cookies 116
Stained Glass Cookies 115
Sugar Cookies 111

Slice & Bake Cookies
Brown Sugar Nutty Rounds 105
Chocolate Refrigerator Cookies 99
Chocolate Pinwheels 100
Cinnamon Refrigerator Cookies 98
Cocoa-Mints 104
Gingerbread Cookies 96
Lemon Refrigerator Cookies 97
Macadamia Nut Krispies 102
Orange Nut Crisps 103